FOOD TRU

3 Books in 1 - The Strategic and Practical Beginner's
Guide to Accompanying You to Build an Effective and
Profitable Plan to Get Your Food and Business Passion
on the Road

Copyright © 2021

Chuck Street

Introduction

Since the early days of humans, food has always been the major source of human energy; hence food can not be separated from human history. The early humans fought and struggled for food, which led to migration from one place to another, wars, and high survival instincts. As the centuries pass, humans started to cultivate the land for farming and rearing of animals to make life easier and don't have to travel distance for a single meal. Eventually, the business aspect came in, people started exchanging one food for another or other goods.

Over time, humans have been devising and innovating sources of food, which has increased exponentially and continued to change over time. While early humans had to go far distance to find their daily meals, nowadays, we are surrounded by several promotions and advertisements for food products of different types, prices, and qualities. This led to the birth of the enormous food industry we have presently.

The food industry has always been a complex and global network that consists of diverse businesses. Most of the food consumed by humans has been supplied by the food industry, and this industry covers a series of production processes:

- Preparation and Production,
- Processing and Distribution,
- Transport and Preservation,
- Certification, Assembling, and Packaging of foodstuffs.

The industry has become wide and broad as the manufacturing ranges from a small business (usually family business) to a large business (usually capital-intensive and highly mechanized industrial processes). The industry discussed in this book will be focused on the Food Truck Industry, which has proven to be the future of the food industry.

Summary

BOOK 1: Starter Guide for Food Truck Business: Key Elements to know, Business plan, Profitability and Strategies

1 The Food Truck is Future of the Food Industry

The food truck is a familiar sight to many if one sees them, perhaps on the street, with a throng of people queuing or through the television with the aim to sell as much of their goods as possible. With the crowds and exposure that a food truck owner gets, it is entirely possible for your thought process to make the connection from "Food Trucks are Nice" to "I want to have a food truck." If you fall under the latter category, then perhaps, it is time for a little dose of reality. On the outside, it may seem like the owner of a food truck has it easy by driving around your town, being able to sell food to hungry crowds, and make easy money off it. This is the culmination of several months or perhaps years of planning that led to that very moment of the epiphany of your desire to want to have a food truck.

As a food truck owner, there are numerous responsibilities that you must handle. There is the need to finance your food truck concept, then search for the perfect truck for your needs and the adjustments needed to reflect your idea. Then there is the search for your ingredient sources, the right staff to handle your food items, and, more importantly, develop ways to make your food truck a sustainable and profitable business.

This chapter is meant to ease you into the world of the food truck industry and make you part of the industry that became a revolution on how one gets their food and how getting delicious food to customers can be easy as parking in the right spot.

What is a Food Truck?

There is no specific definition for a food truck because it is a matter of opinion, even if you try the search engine. It can generally be assumed that a food truck is presumably a truck or any vehicle that has the capacity for preparing and selling a particular type of food in a locale. While this may be true, one can be aware that there are several types of trucks and vehicles to choose from, and one may think that this is an oversimplified definition of what a food truck truly is. However, the impact that food truck has had on the food industry cannot be denied.

How the Food Truck Revolutionized the Food Industry

How did the food truck evolve into a burgeoning industry that rakes in approximately $650 million dollars a year? More importantly, how did food truck businesses become the fastest growing sector of the restaurant industry? It all starts with the idea of street food. One is familiar with the food truck that looks like a motorized truck that comes in highly decorated hues to be more representative of the owner's theme, or maybe in a chrome finish for a more space-age look. While this is the modern food truck, the food truck concept has been around since the 17th century, where street food became a popular idea. The earliest incarnation of the food truck can still be seen today in the form of push carts, as the idea started in New York. Then it evolved to the chuck wagon, which fed the families that populated the American Frontier, and then to carts, which provided convenient food for students in their dormitories. A familiar idea for the food truck comes in the form of the ice cream truck, which became the first modern concept of the food truck when an ice cream truck was retrofitted to become a taco truck. This incarnation of the food truck continued to cater to the needs of students with the ease of access to convenient food. This later on developed into an industry that expanded its repertoire of meals from ones that you could find at a greasy spoon to meals that are more reflective of the culture of the food truck owner. The popularity of the food truck peaked in 2010 with a very familiar show, the Great Food Truck Race, which devoted its focus to the food truck industry.

Because of its burgeoning popularity and the high market for the food truck, the Federal Government of the United States established guidelines for those who wish to establish a street food business. Since this is a guide to get you started on the food truck industry, a quick read would be necessary so you know what to prepare. **www.sba.gov** is the link to see the necessary papers and requirements needed if you contemplate entering the food industry. This link is for the United

States only; other countries will also have their guidelines. Do your research about the guidelines that concern your country's food industry to get the necessary requirements. Once you have your food truck up and running, make sure that your food is consistent and, more importantly, tasty and delicious, as food trucks are now considered review-worthy by the Zagat survey.

1.1   Starting as a Food Truck Owner

When running a food truck, you may be wondering whether the food truck company is a part-time venture or a full-time commitment. However, it is understood that this is a full-time commitment on your part to run a business efficiently.

From the perspective of a food truck owner, if you are an early riser, that might be an advantage, although, after a few shifts on the food truck, your sleep schedule might undergo a few changes. The typical day of the food truck owner begins at 9 am, where the planning process takes place. This includes the need to look at Social Media Accounts to scout for events that you can take advantage of, check out customer reviews on other Social Media platforms, and check other miscellaneous correspondence that has entered your inbox overnight. There is a need to plan your itinerary to ensure that your route (if you have one) is free of any hitches.

There is the need to meet with your team and discuss menu options for the day and areas where your services can improve upon. At this point, you can consider the feedback other members of the team have received from other customers and be aware of what the competition is like out there. This emphasizes the importance of communication, as it is a source of useful information on how to improve and scope out the competition. It also makes your employees believe that their voices are heard and important to you.

Afternoons are usually the prime time for food truck owners to purchase the food supplies needed to make the day's specials, or if you have placed orders with a local commissary that you frequent, locate the shipments and take inventory, a necessary task to ensure that you do not end up wasting food and money. Once the inventory has been taken, it is time for the prep work to facilitate the ease of preparing food in the food truck. This is important as the food truck has limited space to work with, so efficiency in food preparation is a must. An important part of the service now would be Social Media. The afternoon would be the best time to inform customers where your food truck is located at.

Once this is all settled, it is time for the food truck to begin operations at its first stop. Once this happens, the subsequent events would put your resolve to own a food truck to the test. While it is a joy to see frequent customers, there is also that fear where you and your staff are unable to keep up with the demand. After numerous location changes and services, it would be time to close up shop. Don't be deceived with shutting down windows; it is more than that. It also involves the clean-up of the food truck for the next day's service.

If the above sequence of events gives you a thrill, you are certainly in the right business. If you are determined, then this will work for you. One of the necessary traits to have in this business is determination, and this will motivate you every day to make your dream work. Aside from this, you will need to be a hard worker, self-reliant, unafraid of accountability, and a visionary. The food truck business is not a means to obtain easy money, nor is it a means to achieve instant fame. It takes dedication and commitment on your part to make the entire business work.

Is it Possible to Profit from a Food Truck Business?
One of the main concerns for food truck owners is the question of profitability. While owning a food truck does not immediately equate to instant profitability, with the proper planning, marketing, and sales strategies, one can recoup the expenses that went into the preparation for your food truck.

The Hard Side to a Food Truck Business
The food truck may seem to be an easy task to the uninitiated, drive around, cook food, serve, and earn money. However, this is just the

surface veneer of what it takes to be a food truck owner. As one goes through this series, there is more to the food truck business than driving, cooking, and selling. There are certain considerations that one needs to make before making a wholehearted commitment to the food truck business.

- **The Service Rush**
  - Depending on your hours of operation, the operation of a food truck in a lunch or dinner rush, for instance, can make the business seem like a madhouse when you have to deal with a throng of hungry, demanding customers. If you have played games such as Dinner Dash or Cooking Frenzy, or any other multitude of cooking simulation games online, you may have an inkling of what the service rush is about. It also involves getting the orders right, and more importantly, giving these orders to the right customer, all in a reasonable amount of time to prevent impatient customers and potentially negative reviews about your food truck.
- **Maintenance**
  - The food truck, after all, remains a vehicle, although heavily modified to accommodate kitchen equipment, perhaps a bed space or two for the itinerant or more adventurous food truck entrepreneur. Because the food truck is constantly on the go, it has the potential to break down more frequently than a car or any other vehicle. Because of this, the maintenance costs on a food truck can be higher than what you are accustomed to. If the food truck breaks down, this means that income loss is definite. This is a situation that you would want to avoid.
  - Because the food truck breaks down, there is also a question of the employees, who may be disgruntled from the impromptu cancellation of shifts due to the breakdown of the truck, as well as the standing orders

from your food suppliers who have earmarked your specific orders.
  - When a food truck breaks down, it is not only about income loss, it is also about the welfare of your employees and the relationship between your business and your suppliers.

- **Frequent Run-Ins**
  - This is just a more diplomatic way to describe a conflict. As a food truck owner, you will run into your fair share of conflict. This may arise from the owners of nearby restaurants, law enforcement officials, and other food trucks who have established your route as their territory. The food truck business can be quite cutthroat, as despite your best intentions, restaurant owners, for instance, could view your business as a competitor and attempt to find a way to make your food truck move. There is no specific strategy for this except to have your papers ready and, more importantly, maintain a cool head. If you are hot-tempered or easily riled, your temper will have to take a back seat for your business.

- **Trust Issues**
  - Because of the relative size of the food truck, it is virtually impossible to create tiers among your employees. This means that there is no middle ground and certainly no room for a manager to be part of the food truck business, and if you do attempt to hire one, take part in how the food truck is handled. Aside from this, despite your best intentions, there may be the possibility that employees may devise methods to earn a little extra cash on the side through the use of diversion, which can cut into your earnings.

- **Selling Yourself**
  - This is not what it sounds like, but in essence, the food truck and its food are your ideas, so what you really do is selling your idea. However, this requires dedication on

your part as the food truck owner. If you are a natural-born salesperson, this will be to your advantage; if not, make it work. Additionally, because of the lack of managers, it is ideal if you are on-site to ensure that everything goes off without a hitch. However, you do get one advantage here: you sell your idea to the customers and provide recommendations. Your reviews will show this.

- **Miscellaneous Events**
  - o There are a few events that can make you want to throw in the towel, such as your engine not starting, run-ins with police officers, the breakdown of kitchen equipment that slows down your food production, or worse, spoils your food and increases the amount of food waste your business generates, or simple items such as the lack of small change, and nowhere in sight to get more change. A keen eye, constant supervision, and maintenance on your part are enough to offset this potentiality.

How The Food Truck Business Can Be an Advantage

Every business has its pros and cons, and it is best to understand both. Running a food truck business can come with many advantages, and those potential events aside from your food truck business or the idea of it can net you several advantages.

- **Satisfaction**
  - o This is satisfaction felt on both sides of the food truck. On your part, it's the thrill that keeps you motivated when a customer leaves happy, or better, exclaims that your food is absolutely delicious and will keep coming back for more. On the customer's part, it's the thrill of discovery and the enjoyment of the food every time they return.

- **The Culmination of an Idea**
  - o Earlier in this chapter, it was mentioned that the food truck is a representation of your idea. It does not have

to be culturally based, but it is an idea that you feel you want to share with the public and hopefully make a living. Because the food you sell reflects your idea, there is the enjoyment of the knowledge that your food and your idea. Additionally, you can tweak it to reflect more of your personality; after all, it is your food truck, and you are the boss.

- **Building Up**
  - This will be elaborated on later in the book, but building up entails creating a brand that people will come to associate with you. Aside from this, if you enjoy food and are trying to break into the food industry, this would be the best means to go about it if you do not have the financial capacity for an actual premises. This could be a stepping stone to a restaurant of your own if potential investors see a high demand for your product. Just think of the movie **Chef;** the ending scene lends credence to this scenario.
- **Break Free**
  - If you have felt burned out in your previous career, the food truck can be the relief you need because you are in control of your time and almost everything else. What can be more euphoric than giving directions instead of being given directions? Additionally, because you are on wheels, you get more freedom to move about, and because you open at a time you choose, you have better control of your time.
  - This also gives you additional satisfaction over your ability to control how your ideas are managed and the enjoyment that you created a career for those who need it - an important concept, with consideration to the impact the COVID-19 Pandemic has caused.

1.2 The Many Forms of a Food Truck

Earlier in the chapter, there was a brief overview of how the food truck came to be, and while some forms of it still exist (i.e. food carts), you certainly will not find chuck wagons meandering through the streets. If a truck is not your thing, there are several options for you to consider before we get into the nitty-gritty of the food truck business.

- **Food Carts**
  - The food cart, as mentioned earlier, is the earliest form of the food truck and is still quite visible even today. In New York, for instance, those hotdog carts that sell an Authentic NY Style Hotdog in a Bun are the best examples of a food cart, although there are more elaborate versions about it. Remember, to succeed in the business, you need to stand out. Food carts regularly dish out street food and are generally inexpensive due to the low costs it has.
  - You can expect food carts to have some form of license to operate and, like other forms of the food truck, can capitalize on events within the vicinity. For the safety and assurance of everyone, it would be a good idea to have an updated food safety certificate, which will be discussed later.

- **Concession Stands**
  - A concession stand, albeit a mobile one, differs from most food trucks because it offers items that are generally found in a movie theater. Though these are generally unhealthy options (yet still equally delicious), it is possible to offer healthier alternatives to ensure that your "concession stand" still stands out.
  - Alternatively, this could save on preparation costs and additional equipment as you can sell pre-made items such as baked goods on-site or simpler items such as drinks and candy bars.

- o If you would like to add additional impact to the concession stand, items that require cooking can be sold. Though, traditionally, the concession stand deals with snack items, popular items that include pizza, fries, nachos, and hotdogs retain their popularity with the crowd.

- **Booths**
  - o A food truck can also take the form of a booth that can cater to specific events. The idea for the booth is that the food is set up and customers can choose what they would like to order. Alternatively, for private engagements that your food truck caters to, pre-set and pre-paid menus are set up where the guests can linger around the food truck and eat. In addition, this is a fantastic method to increase your company's visibility.

- **Gourmet Trucks**
  - o While food trucks are traditionally and by reputation sell street food items from all over the world, according to your selected theme, the gourmet food truck sets itself above the rest through the integration of fine dining concepts and more unique fusion cuisines one would find at a restaurant.

- **Kogi-BBQ Food Truck**
  - o It would be remiss not to mention one of the more famous food trucks, the Kogi-BBQ food truck, that made its mark on the industry with its take on Korean-Mexican fusion cuisine.

- **Bustaurants**
  - o The first bus restaurant in the United States, World Fare, uses a double-decker bus as a food truck and notifies its customers about its location through Twitter. The bustaurant takes orders from the lower tier of the

bus, and because of the display windows, which provides great transparency and insight to the customers to see how their food is, there is greater interaction.

- ○ Additionally, unlike other food trucks where the customer stands up while eating the food, the bustaurant is exactly what it sounds like, a restaurant on a bus. The customer can sit and enjoy their food at leisure. The bustaurant does not move from its location all the time to avoid motion sickness for the customers, among other issues. World Fare, for instance, uses the second tier of its bus as a seating area with panoramic views of Los Angeles.
- ○ If you have more ambition, the necessary background, and, more importantly, the funds, the bus restaurant is as close to a bricks-and-mortar restaurant with the allure and convenience of the food truck business.
- ○ Other food truck themes can be thematic because they use a single ingredient and make it the star of their multiple food items. Bananas, Waffles, Bacon, Crepes, Empanadas, the only limit is how many ways you can interpret a single ingredient and make it more appealing to the crowd.

1.3   Conclusion

The food truck business is an industry that revolutionized how customers can obtain their food, whether it is a simple hotdog with all the toppings or a gourmet feast worthy of a restaurant. The food truck has come far from its humble origins as a food cart that dispensed street food in the 17th century, and now it is a multi-million dollar industry that you want to break into.

The life of a food truck owner is fraught with numerous issues, including the need to come up with plans, put up with long nights, potential staff issues, but the joy and the satisfaction you get when you hear customers rave about your food is well worth the effort you invested into your food truck. Owning a food truck requires wholehearted commitment on your part for it to be a success. Success does not come overnight, and as long as you prepare for any eventuality and maintain your food truck in its optimal state, then owning a food truck will be a breeze.

There are several forms a food truck can take, but this is dependent on your finances and your capabilities to manage. More important to the food truck is the idea behind it, and how you package your idea into an item that will sell and net you profit. The future of the food industry lies in the food truck business, and the next chapter guides you on the tedious task of planning your food truck.

2 Planning a Food Truck Business

Before the planning process starts, there are a few considerations that need to be made:

- Do you intend to make the food truck a full-time or a part-time career?
- How much will the food truck business have to earn to sustain your needs?
- What are the items that you intend to have on offer?
- How do you envision your food truck business?
- What are the schedules that you have in mind for your food truck business?

Once you have answered these questions and have a general idea for your food truck, you can begin work on the business plan that you will need to present to potential investors and financers, as well as the necessary licensing authorities.

2.1 The Business Plan

Consider the business plan a necessary task for your food truck business to take off. It is an important document that enables you to obtain the finances that you need to get your food truck started. Even if you may be independently wealthy, a business plan is a good idea as it helps you anticipate potential problems, as well as potential earnings. It has the added advantage or compulsion to make you stay within a budget. You will need to familiarize yourself with several terms because a business plan requires some background knowledge in accounting.

- **Balance Sheet**

  A balance sheet provides you with a clearer picture of the finance of your business. It provides an outline of your assets, liabilities, and capital.

  Assets – are valuable items in your business; they are usually listed on the balance sheet in accordance with their value, with the most valuable asset at the top and the least valuable asset at the end of the list. Examples of assets are savings, money that is due to you, such as payments that are pending, and, more importantly, the inventory of items that are yet to be sold.

  Liabilities – do not sound so bad. These are the obligations that your business owes, usually listed according to how soon the due date of the obligation is. These can usually take the form of accounts that you have to pay your suppliers, taxes, and loans that you may have taken out.

  Capital – simply, this is the amount of money you and your investors put at stake for the business.

- **Cash Flow Statement**

  This statement enables you to track any changes in your accounts over time, enabling you to identify if you are gaining money or losing money in your business.

  Operating – This is defined as the amount of cash you have with the expenses subtracted from the total amount of sales you made. This is a key area to keep an eye on as this must always be on the positive side. Negative means that your business operates at a loss.

Investing – These are expenses necessary to your business, for instance, the purchase of equipment.

Financing – These are cash that is received from investors or bank loans are taken out prior to the start of the business.

- **Income Statement**
  This statement helps you identify how well your business performs. It highlights what was earned and the necessary costs that made the earnings. This is often formatted in the following manner: Revenue, Cost of Goods Sold, Gross Profit, Labor Costs, Operations Costs, Occupancy Costs, Management Costs, Net Income.
- **Variable Costs**
  Are defined as costs that pertain to the sales of the business. For instance, the costs for food purchases and the necessary items to serve them, as they change.
- **Fixed Costs**
  Are costs that are not dependent on the amount of sales generated; these usually include bills, salaries, and leases.
- **Sunk Costs**
  Though generally irrelevant to the business, these are unrecoverable expenses.

What is Needed in a Basic Business Plan?

There are two formats to a business plan which can be adjusted to the projected needs of your company. These are called the traditional method – more detail-oriented and would work best, and the lean or start-up method – provides an overview of your plans.

Regardless of the approach used, the following are always included in business plans: A market analysis, the marketing strategies, an executive summary, a company description, , the organisation and management, the products and a request for funds, which must include financial projections.

A Template of a Basic Business Plan

Since there are two formats that you can use to create a business plan, the subsequent subheadings play their role to convince investors that your food truck business is a good idea to finance or at least support.

An Executive Summary

An executive summary tells the reader of the business plan about your company and how it will be successful (use will – this signifies determination on your part). Traditional executive summaries include the mission statements of your company (which does not need to be elaborate, a simple sentence would do), the products, and services. The basic information in the executive summary includes the leadership team, employees and if you have envisioned a particular route for your food truck business, include that. Financial information and plans for growth are a must if this business plan includes a financial request.

A Brief Description of Your Idea

Simply put, this is the company description. In the food truck business, you will want to describe your company in detail and the niche that it intends to fill in the food truck industry. Identify the clientele that your food truck business targets and include the advantages that your business has over similarly themed competitors.

Products and Services

While not a category in itself, this is an important area to concentrate on for the food truck business. Here, describe the menu and the concepts behind it. This is also a chance to showcase how well you prepared through the presentation of food costs and market analysis. A few samples to give to the investor would not go amiss either.

Industry Analysis

Essentially the same as market analysis, this area should provide an insight into how the food truck business prospers in your area. A bit of research into your area's regulations on mobile business needs to be presented here.

Competitive Analysis

This is a chance for you to scope out your competition and detail how your food truck differs from these competitors, such as the use of the design to make your food truck stand out, how your food differs from the food sold by other competitors, why you chose the specific route for your food truck, and what makes your food concept a truly unique concept from other food trucks.

Organization and Management

If you have a team set up for your business, the details about your team and management setup are to be detailed in this part of the business plan. To gain an advantage here, remember that investors are more apt to consider those who have experience in the industry and a history of successes in business.

Marketing and Sales

Describe your marketing strategies for your food truck business. Do you plan on the frequent use of social media? Or are there other strategies you plan on. Regardless, if your company has a social media handle, be sure to include it.

Financial Plans (Funding Requests and Financial Projections)

This details the costs needed to open the business and your expectations as to how well your business will perform. This is the time you consider seasonality because you will need to detail how you plan to keep your business afloat during the slowest months of the year, and a monthly breakdown of your plans would be a good idea.

Because this area relates to finances, and this plan would need to court investors, this area also details the amount of money your business will need. Financial projections reassure the investor that your business is a good idea, and documentation would help bolster their confidence in your business: specify predicted income statements, cash flow statements, and capital expenditure budgets.

Fund requests require another set of documentation that should be added to the appendix of the business plan, and these include the costs to purchase equipment and materials, salaries, how bills will be paid until the food truck begins to earn, and plans to fall back on, such as debt payment.

2.2 Concepts

Your food truck business concept is central to the business plan that you intend to draft for potential investors. This is the core of your business, and when you know what your concept is, the remainder of the ideas will follow suit and ease the path for your business plan. The only exception for the need for a concept is if you happen to be the franchisee of an existing food truck business.

There are several concepts to choose from, and some of the more popular food truck themes in the United States include items such as Barbecue, Cupcakes, Waffles, Sandwiches, Burgers, and Paninis. In the first chapter, we discussed the various forms that food trucks can take. In this section, we will continue by talking about the products that aim to make your food truck a successful enterprise. Knowing your concept helps develop the identity of your food truck business and helps customers remember what your food truck is known for.

While there are sweet and savory options to choose from as themes, there needs to be some diversification. Some of the more popular options are in the list below:

- **American cuisine** – which in turn includes food from Regional American Cuisine; for this kind of concept, you can expect burgers, barbecues, and pies. We also have the Regional Specialty Items, such as clam chowder and po'boys.

- **Mexican cuisine** – Mexican cuisine is quite diverse due to the numerous types of regional fare offered in each state in Mexico. There are familiar options such as burritos, enchiladas, and tacos, but there are also other options such as chile rellenos. If you have a family recipe with unique Mexican dishes, a food truck would be a nice way to introduce the public to your take on Mexican Regional Specialties.

- **Italian cuisine** – perhaps a more familiar sight with all the pizzas, pastas, and Panini sandwiches. However, if one looks at Italian street food, there are other delectable options such as zeppole (Italian-style doughnut holes) and arancini (deep-fried risotto balls stuffed with cheese).

- **Mediterranean cuisine** – The Mediterranean is a very broad region to choose from, so cuisines here can run the gamut from Spanish tapas to Lebanese Hummus. Because of this, you will need to do some research as to what you feel your customers would like. If they like burritos, they would like the Greek Gyros, which are almost the same idea, but with a Greek twist. Falafel is a good idea, and so are other Pita sandwiches with varied fillings.

- **Asian cuisine** – is difficult to categorize into a singular cuisine as there are several cuisines enfolded within its definition. Here are some of a few choices:
    - o **Vietnamese cuisine** – Vietnamese cuisine is an enticing hybrid of Asian flavors melded with French techniques. If noodles are a thing, Pho is a good idea, and if sandwiches are a hit, you cannot go wrong with a Banh Mi Sandwich, which may appeal to all those pulled pork sandwich lovers in public.
    - o **Japanese cuisine** – Most Japanese themes include Sushi as a theme, but this can be diversified into other Japanese delicacies such as Takoyaki, Donburi Rice Meals, Bento Boxes, and the ever-popular Tempura-style dishes.
    - o **Korean cuisine** – seems to be a hit, given the success story of the Kogi BBQ Food Trucks of Chef Roy Choi. There are also other Korean dishes that can be offered to the public, as well as desserts that feature matcha.
    - o **Chinese cuisine** – perhaps the most familiar of the Asian Cuisines. There are numerous forms of dishes that customers can choose from, such as noodles, dim sum, dumplings, egg rolls, spring rolls, and Jianbing. The one concern here is that most of the dishes can have soy elements that many are allergic to, so a warning on the menu would not go amiss. Salt may be an issue with customers as well, so it is important to find a balance with flavor.
    - o **Indian cuisine** – Who doesn't love flatbreads and curry? The spice and evocative scents would draw customers to your food truck before you can do anything else. Aside from this, Tandoori Chicken,

Mutton Curry, and Butter Chicken are just a few of the many dishes that you can sell from this specific theme.

- An advantage that could be had is that many Asian cuisines have dishes that are centered around vegetables as a core ingredient. Use this advantage to draw in the vegetarian crowds, to give them more options to choose from.

- **Desserts** —a dessert truck is a viable option, and there is more to this than selling ice cream. Specialty cookies, brownies, hand pies, cannolis, Belgian waffles are a big draw for crowds. Dessert trucks can also integrate ethnic cuisines such as Baklava (a Greek dessert made of phyllo pastry, layered with nuts and honey), Cannoli, and Sopaipillas.

Your food truck's idea gives your company an identity, and as a result, it will make your business plan more concrete and increase the probability of attracting investors. While it is entirely okay to go with the suggested ideas under this area, feel free to make the food truck your own. After all, the above ideas are just the demographic, and what is important is that your business stands out.

What Do You Intend Your Business to Achieve

Ask yourself this once you have crafted your concept for the food truck: Is your concept unique enough to warrant a market for your food items? Can people easily understand what your food truck is all about? Why?

A unique concept helps your food truck stand out more from several others like it and other similarly themed restaurants as well. Take this scenario: You want to open a food truck that sells ice cream, for instance, and there are other ice cream food trucks in the neighbourhood; you will need to step up your game and make a completely unique idea that will draw people to your food truck. This can be achieved by using fusion cuisine (which works well with savory dishes) or using a specific core ingredient (which works for both sweet and savory dishes).

If you binge-watch a few episodes of the Great Food Truck Race, you will see unique concepts such as a macaroni and cheese truck, a gourmet restaurant-style food truck, brunch food trucks, and vegan food trucks. It all depends on how you interpret your idea into your cooking. Ultimately, the food is the big draw.

Unique ideas need a unique presentation, so the outside of your food truck will have to reflect on what your concept is. For your food to sell, you need to be visible. If you want to sell cupcakes, make the exterior look like a cupcake. If you sell sandwiches, put a sandwich in your logo. This is a discussion that will be elaborated on in the Chapter on Branding. The point is that your customers immediately understand what you are selling. You don't want anything obscure. This also reflects upon your investors, who need to understand that what you are promoting is a good idea.

The information that you come up with here should form part of the executive summary.

Preparation is Key: Documentation is Always a Good Idea

This section will list down the various attachments that you can append to your business plan to bolster the assurance that your business is a good idea.

- A Sample Menu of your planned food items
- Photos of the Products from the Sample Menu attached to the Business Plan
- Permits from the Necessary Authorities (More on this later on)
- Letters of Reference (For this one, you will need references from persons who are not related to you, and it would be better to obtain this from people who have backgrounds in the food industry and business)
- Financial Documents
  o A monthly breakdown of your plans for the food truck, with clear ideas on how you plan to keep your food truck earning each month, and plans for slow months for your food truck.
  o Predictive Income Statements
  o Cash Flow Statements
  o Capital Expenditure Budgets

- Prices of the Equipment You will need for your food truck
- Social Media Handles

Is There a Market for Your Idea?

One of the more important tasks for a food truck owner is analysis, which helps reassure investors and banks that your food truck is a business worth their investment. There are two types of analysis mentioned as part of the business plan: Industry Analysis and Competitive Analysis.

Why would you need to do this? At the heart of it all, business is a matter of competition, and despite the friendliness of it all, the food truck business aims to sell, and you will need to learn more about the other food trucks and food establishments in your area to know if your business is a viable idea.

Competition is a necessary aspect of any business, as it gives you the opportunity to continually improve your business and get creative with how you market your business. Though competition may give the compulsion to change prices, you will need to strike a balance and make reasonable prices for your products.

- **Competitive Analysis**
    - This takes time to accomplish as you will need to be thorough in how you gather data from other food trucks and food establishments.
    - Comparison is necessary, and you will need to create a summary of these businesses, what their menus offer to the public, how their items are priced, and their target population.
    - Through this, you can identify the niche that your food truck can fill and be assured that this niche remains unique.

- **Industry Analysis**
    - Industry analysis enables prospective food truck owners to understand how their food truck idea fits in with the other food trucks in the business.

     o   Because you will understand your competitors'
         operations, this will lead to the efficient creation of
         marketing strategies for your business.

There is a specific cycle referred to in the business sector as the
competitive response cycle. This cycle helps ensure that your food
truck remains a relevant business and can meet the needs and demands
of your customers. The said cycle involves the following steps:

- Analyze what your customers want and what they need from your food truck.
- Analyze your competitors and see how they fulfill their customers' wants and needs.
- Identify a way your business can fulfill the customers' needs and take care of the wants that your competitors were not able to.
- Create programs that will take advantage of these opportunities to answer the needs and wants of customers.
- Evaluate the response of your customers to your method of fulfilling their needs and wants.

Know Your Demographic

Important to the food truck business is the identification of your target
audience. While it can be easy to say that just choosing an area with
heavy foot traffic is not always the case because your food truck may
not be to everyone's tastes. Demographics refer to the characteristics of
customers who you feel are more likely to purchase from your food
truck. These data include the age group, income status, educational
status, occupation, and household size.

- You will need to know what genders usually frequent the food truck idea that you have.
- Identify a specific age group that you would like to target (College-Age, Young Adult, etc.)
- The educational status of your customers
  - o   Not to discriminate, but mind you, this is to ensure that your products will appeal to the right customer. A gourmet food truck is not going to work well with people who are unfamiliar or cannot understand the

concept of what your food truck is. Likewise, a simple food truck with a simple idea might be too plebeian to customers who look for more elaborate food.

- Your ideal customer's locale
  - You will want to identify an ideal location for your food truck. For instance, you sell Asian food; you will want to place your food truck at a location with a large Asian population.
- Their occupation
  - Sometimes, the occupation matters. Assuming they are medical professionals (to include other hospital workers), a hearty meal from a food truck can revive them more than a dessert food truck.
- The income status
  - Again, not to discern, but to ensure that your offerings in the food truck are ideal for the right customers. Those with a higher income status are more likely to purchase more expensive food items and go for a food truck that has a more cosmopolitan selection. Alternately, a food truck that sells the more common (yet equally delicious) dishes appeals more to low-income families.

Once you have identified your ideal clientele, you can make adjustments to your theme to fit the specifications of your business plan. Additionally, the inclusion of this information in your business plan will prove that you did do your research and the necessary analyses that would help lend credence to your idea.

2.3   The Cost of Running a Food Truck

Before you consolidate your business plans to present to investors, you will need to identify the costs that will be undertaken once your food truck opens to the public. These include the costs to open the food truck and the predicted earnings for your food truck. Additionally, these form part of the requirements needed for the business plan to prove that your idea is financially capable of recouping the investments made into your business.

Opening Costs

Generally, the opening costs are the same costs that are present when you open your food truck for business. This details how much you will need to be able to get your business started. These include the costs for food and supplies and labor expenses incurred before the food truck officially opens for business. Remember that in the training period before the food truck opens, you will need to train your staff on how to prepare the meals and the other miscellaneous items. The average opening cost for a food truck ranges from $30,000 to $80,000. This is not a consolidated figure because you would have to know if you would like to purchase or simply rent your food truck.

It is entirely possible to open a food truck with smaller costs through renting one, which gives you enough of a budget to brand the food truck, establish a relationship with a commissary and provide an initial payment, purchase the items needed for opening day, train the staff and create an online presence. However, it would also be good to consider the costs of purchasing a truck outright, though it may be the more expensive option.

If you rent a vehicle, $50,000 is a fair price to start a food truck company. If you decide to use a used food truck, this projected figure doubles. If you choose a brand-new food truck, it quadruples. This, however, should be researched just like everything else in the business plan. This is because of the inevitable change in price, which eventually changes the costs, and it might be possible that the opening costs could be lower due to low demand, or vice versa. A good strategy to prevent overshooting the budget would involve a 10% increase on all the prices, just to ensure you have enough room to maneuver once the time to purchase comes.

Modeling Revenue

Contrary to what it sounds, this does not have anything to do with the exterior and aesthetics of the truck. This refers to the predictive costs that need to be made, so in essence, this is all theoretical. There are several steps that need to be taken with regards to the estimation of costs, one of which you may have already done if you did an industry analysis and observed other food truck businesses as well as restaurants that have a large following.

If you did the industry analysis, you need to identify what makes these food establishments prosper in the area that you intend to establish your food truck in. Speak with the owners whenever possible; some of them may be happy to share the tools of the trade and the inside scoop on the area. You will need to identify how many customers frequent a specific food truck to be able to gain a reasonable estimate as to how many potential sales your food truck can generate.

There are two types of calculations that factor into the prediction of revenue, and these are called the Top-Down and Bottom-Up Calculations.

- **Top-Down Calculations**

   This requires a look at how franchises operate to determine how well a particular theme performs in a specific area. You will want to identify food trucks with a similar theme and gauge how well these food trucks perform in the said business. For instance, if you would like to sell desserts, check out how other dessert shops in the area perform, or if a specific cultural cuisine, identify if they are doing well. If they are doing well, then the food truck idea would do well as it approximately earns 20 to 40 percent more than a brick and mortar establishment.

- **Bottom-Up Calculations**

   The Bottom-Up Calculations requires a specific formula to determine how many potential sales can be made. This is called bottom-up calculations, and this is best computed from the time the item is made to the time it is sold.

   This is computed with the formula: average sales per guest x number of expected guests per day.

   This highlights the need for the industry analysis to gain an accurate picture of how many customers regularly frequent a food truck. Through this formula, it is also entirely possible to compute the number of sales made per hour. To compute the number of sales per hour, utilize the same formula but consider the number of expected customers for that specific period.

Aside from these two computations, there are several more costs to be considered once the food truck is fully operational. This involves the Cost of Goods Sold and the computation of the Gross Profit once the Labor, Operating Costs, Occupancy Costs, Management Costs, and Net Income have been taken into consideration.

Cost of Goods Sold

The cost of products sold industry average is estimated to be around 30%. The cost of products sold is based on your product; therefore, this is not a constant proportion. For example, the prices of grilled cheese sandwiches will be modest, but if you intend on other higher-end meals, the costs of products sold will have to rise. This is best computed using the bottom-up computation and adding 5% to account for food wastage.

Labor Costs

This is simply the salaries of your employees, which is approximately 30 percent and also following the usual industry standards. The labor cost is commensurate to the amount of experience your employees have. A seasoned chef would have to be paid considerably more when contrasted with a cook, for instance.

The labor cost is best estimated with the bottom-up computation, where you need to take into account the number of employees needed in a single shift and the number of shifts in a day. Multiply with the prevailing wage in your area, and include the payroll taxes in your computation (which accounts from 10-12 percent), then divide the labor costs by sales in a particular period.

Operating Costs

These are the general operating expenses needed for the food truck to work, which entails every item that does not involve food and food service. Aside from this, operational costs include the professional fees of lawyers, accountants, webmasters (if you have a website), and a graphic designer.

Occupancy Costs

Just because you are in a food truck does not mean you are free from rent. The usual occupancy cost for a brick and mortar establishment would run them about 8-10 percent, higher if these restaurants are in an urban area. The occupancy cost for a food truck is significantly lower than this, though it cannot be eliminated as food trucks still utilize parking space, for instance, at a food truck park. There are also event fees, fuel, and parking tickets (just try to avoid these as much as possible). Because of these costs, occupancy costs can take up from 7 to 10 percent of total sales made in the food truck.

Do some reconnaissance and scope out the usual fees for the space you intend to use, as well as rental costs for additional equipment, commissaries, and a kitchen, if need be. It would be a good idea to set aside a part of the total sales for the event fees where you can provide the food.

Management Costs

In order to make your food truck company run well, here are the expenses involved, and here is how you calculate your pay. Most likely, your payment will be paid partially from the management expenses and partly from the labor costs.

Net Income

A daily budget that would nail you at least 10 percent profit is a good place to start with your daily plans. If you are not math savvy, obtain the help of an accountant or a bookkeeper to ensure that your accounting is correct because taxes, interest, and depreciation may be overlooked in your zeal to identify the total income earned.

Why Seasons Are Important for the Food Truck Beginner

This refers to the term of seasonality, which forms part of the business plan, and part of your overall plan in your food truck business operation, as it determines how much potential sales can be made at a specific time and how your cash flow is affected. For certain places that experience winters and thus are classified as seasonal markets, the food truck business may have very little chance to operate. For those who serve any frozen items, the winter season would cause the business to halt, while conversely, the summer season would cause the frozen items to boom.

Because seasonality affects business, you will need to consider the upkeep of the food truck while it is in storage, or, if you brave the cold (in the assumption that it is winter), the maintenance and the items needed to winterize the food truck. If you live in an area with little to no snow, seasonality will focus on the best times to sell your food. This forms an important part of your business plan as well, as you will need to detail to investors how your food truck business can earn during the slowest months of operation. This requires the creation of the monthly breakdown to ensure that your business remains a viable option.

Raising the Capital

Once the business plan is crafted, the next concern for the food truck business involves the capital to start up the food truck business. If you are financially independent, you will want to skip this section. If not, there are several methods that can be used to obtain the funds needed to make your dreams a reality.

Various Means to Raise the Capital Needed for Your Food Truck

There are three types of capital that can be raised for the food truck business:

1. **Seed Capital** refers to the money needed if the analyses and creation of your plans require it. This type of capital is best utilized if you plan to operate more than a single food truck. This is not ideal for you if you plan to operate a single food truck, as the analyses and plans are relatively cheaper when compared to multiple food trucks.

2. **Start-Up Capital** is the capital that helps you with the purchase of the equipment your food truck business needs, the rent for the space, supplies you will need for your food items, and other miscellaneous expenses for the first operational year of your food truck.

3. **Expansion Capital** is the money that is meant to help your business increase or improve. Expansion capital may be used to purchase better equipment for the food truck or simply to add another food truck to your food truck business (if you are established).

To decide what quantity of money you'll require, you'll have to evaluate what form of capital you'll need and the ways of generating cash you'll be able to use. Start-up funding may not be required because research may be conducted cheaply. On the other hand, expansion capital is of little use to someone who is just getting started. So far, the costs for your business have been presented, and to determine how much capital you will need, you will need to determine your entire business cost. Recurring expenditures include things like buying the food supply, which you'll repeatedly need (such as the purchase of insurance for your food truck). Therefore, it is necessary to research how much each item on your list will cost. Research is needed to determine how much each specific item on your list will cost. A good strategy would be to identify how much is needed for your one-time costs and plan your budget around the recurrent costs for your monthly expenses.

One-Time Costs	Recurrent Costs
The Food Truck	Insurance
Retrofitting the Truck	Rent for a Commercial Kitchen (optional)
Licenses and Permits	Payroll (Salaries)
Consultation Fees	Card Processing Equipment
Initial Food Supplies and Kitchen Equipment	Maintenance Costs
Website Design	Miscellaneous Expenses (give
Advertisement and PR	yourself room to maneuver with a contingency fee of 5% at least)

Save for the Rainy Day with a Reserve Fund

Reserve some funds for the operation of your food truck for at least a year into the operation. Despite your efforts at advertisements, the research, and the analysis performed in the course of the creation of your business plan, it is never guaranteed that your food truck will be an instant hit. When this happens, the reserve fund comes in handy to ensure that your business can stay afloat while it establishes itself. When socking away money for your reserve fund, take into consideration increases in costs, particularly for labor, supplies, licenses, and event fees.

Predict these expenses through the use of the modeling revenue earlier in the chapter to identify other potential expenses that may arise in the first year of the food truck's operation.

Personal Funds

It was mentioned in the previous chapter that the operation of the food truck requires commitment, and this section deals with the commitment of your personal funds towards the establishment of your business. If you hear the expression put your money where your mouth is, then this is the right context to apply it in. Investors are more likely to invest in an idea that you have personally invested in. If you can establish a food truck with personal funds, you can retain full control and ownership over the food truck. This requires the use of loans, credit cards, and other financial assets you may have.

Statistically, 50 percent of small businesses are established with the use of personal funds. Because you invested in yourself using personal funds, future loans will be easier as you have proven that you can finance a business yourself. The main disadvantage with the use of personal funds is that in the event your business fails, there is the potential to lose your investment and any collateral used to secure loans. The use of personal funds is ideal if you have a low start-up cost and if you pay smaller fees for the miscellaneous paperwork needed for your food truck to operate. This is best identified with the start-up costs list that was described in this chapter.

There are several ways to use personal funds:

The use of **personal savings** is one of the ways to finance your truck. However, if the business does not take off, you can lose your investment. It is a risk, but it also saves you from the hefty interest that comes with loans.

The **401k** or your nest egg would require you to risk your retirement savings (if you have one). However, in accordance with the laws on the use of retirement accounts, you will have to check out regulations and laws In your country to determine how to turn your 401k into a corporate retirement account that allows you to invest the stored funds into your business. This involves moving the 401k into a profit-sharing plan for your company, which converts it into a corporate account that belongs to the company, not solely yours.

Home Equity Loans are a way for you to secure funds with minimal risk, as banks do not need to know where the money is invested in since there is collateral for them to assure that they can get their loan back.

Personal Loans ensure that your food truck business remains in your sole ownership. Because this is a personal loan, you will have to inform the lender of the loan's purposes, which may require the presentation of the business plan that you have crafted.

Credit Cards, though personal, carry a great deal of risk since they were never meant to be used for large-scale business investments. However, they serve as a useful bridge for the gap between the time you obtain your start-up capital and the time your business begins operations. A certain degree of caution is needed for this option as a close eye will have to be taken upon the interest rates, additional fees, and late payment fees.

Personal funds may ensure that you control your business, but there is a lot at stake: your savings, your home, and your credit rating. Because of this, consider the use of personal funds if you are not placing yourself or your family in financial jeopardy. Consult with a financial advisor on the potential of a successful loan so that you can obtain a more professional and experienced outlook on the probabilities of your business. You may be able to obtain an additional source of funds.

Friends and Family

This is an unorthodox means to obtain the capital you need to set up the food truck. It is not an easy task to ask your friends and family for the money you need to do this, and more often than not, borrowed money can often lead to the end of a relationship. If this is the path you intend to take, ensure that there is proper documentation for everything to let them know where the money went, and consider the amount that you need to borrow. Be sure it is an amount that you know you can pay back. Consider what will happen to your relationship if you are unable to pay them back at the terms you agreed on. If you feel it won't survive, this is not the best option for you.

Crowdsourcing

An entirely novel concept to obtain the necessary funds for the food truck; this involves incremental amounts of money obtained from many people (the crowd) who are your investors. There are numerous crowdsourcing websites out there to place your business on; Kickstarter and Prosper are good places to start. If you choose to do this, it would be best to create tiers of investment. For instance, basic investment packages will net the investor this. Advanced and Higher tier packages include the items with the basic investment package as well as a few additional perks to make their investment worthwhile. If you are familiar with Patreon, this works the same way.

Loans

Financing your company using this option appears to be the most obvious choice, given the possibilities you have; thus, you will need to choose what type of loan you are looking for. When it comes to setting conditions for repayment of a loan, you must mention the loan repayment in your company plan's financials section. First, you will need to know what kind of loans you can apply for.

- **Debt Capital** involves a business loan that you have to pay back over a set period, and as with loans, this involves interest and additional charges. You do, however, remain the sole owner, just with a loan that you need to pay back. Consider if you have good credit and if you can pay the monthly installments on time. You need to consider if the loan provider will be likely to lend you money in the future.
  - For debt capitals, you will need to outline where the money is to be spent. A budget would be useful to prove this. Set the terms that are beneficial for you and your business. Identify the items that you will need as collateral for the needed loan.
- **Equity Capital** does not make you the sole owner anymore as the individual or firms that provided the money obtain a stake in your business to ensure a return on their investment. Consider if you want to give partial control to these third parties.

- There are **General Partners** who take part in how your food truck business is run and share in the profits. These partners share in the debts that the partnership may incur, and they could also lose their investment if the business fails.
- **Limited Partners** do not take part in the business and can only recoup what amount they have invested in your food truck.
- **Silent Partners** are those who invest in the food truck and share in its profits. The silence comes from not taking part in the running of the food truck and retaining liability over the food truck's debts.

Bank Loans

A bank is a question that contradicts because advertisements tell you that loans are easy, but once applied for, you are asked to prove your financials. This is because banks, though good sources of investment, remain skeptical about the food truck business in the belief that this is a trend that will disappear over time. You need to prove that your business is profitable before a bank lends you any money, and they require collateral for asset-backed borrowing. For a bank loan, you do not need to prove the potential of your idea; the bottom line is they want to know if you can pay their money back. More often than not, you will be asked for someone to cosign, and this person must have a good credit rating for this to work.

Because banks have the professional veneer, present yourself as such. Set an appointment with your preferred bank. Be professional in how you act, look, carry yourself, and in the preparation of your business plans and financial documents. Banks are known to ask questions, so keep a cool head and play it cool. Desperation is never a good emotion to show to a loan officer.

What's the SBA?

The Small Business Administration (SBA) is essentially a government agency that serves as a guarantor to banks for the loan you will need, which increases the likelihood that you are able to pay back the loan made. Even if you are unable to meet the terms, the SBA guarantees the bank that it will pay off a percentage of the loan made by you. Since the food truck's start-up costs are relatively low, approximately $200,000, the SBA guarantees 75 percent of your loan with the bank for an amount this low.

Aside from this, the SBA offers Microloan options, where the amounts, up to $35,000, are paid over six years. The loan application made is sent to their affiliate lender, who then waits for the final decision from their bank or credit union.

Because this is a government agency, it is expected that there is a lot of paperwork needed, so this will take some time to accomplish despite the benefits that could be attained when you obtain their help.

2.4 Conclusion

For the food truck business to succeed, plans are essential to ensure that your food truck business and your idea go off to a great start. A business plan is essential for success, and in that, you need to identify the soul of your food truck. A concept solidifies your idea for the food truck and enables you to predict the potential revenues your food truck may earn. Research is key for every other step because preparation with every aspect ensures greater success for your food truck dream to succeed.

3   Food Truck Profitability Demystified

One of the key takeaways from the previous chapter would be the estimation of costs, specifically start-up costs for your food truck to receive the funding it needs. Among the expenses discussed would be the estimation of costs on how much initial inventory is to be purchased as well as the labor costs involved. This chapter provides insight into how a food truck owner manages to earn despite the long list of expenses involved in running a food truck.

Ways of make money

There are several traits that a food truck owner must imbibe to make a food truck a success, one of which is the commitment needed, the funds that help the food truck function, and, more importantly, the expertise that is needed to make the food truck a successful venture. Expertise in this context can be interpreted in different ways. For instance, if you have the funds, the equipment, and the idea, the expertise you will need is a chef or cook who can pull off your idea. In contrast, if you are a chef, cook, or a home cook, you will need someone who can help manage your business effectively to keep it successful.

These are abstract concepts that lead to success; however, what is important is the ability of the food truck to earn, and this is best visualized with how much money the food truck earns in a day, month, and year for it to be considered a success.

Estimation of Costs is Key

Because money is a key aspect in whether or not a food truck succeeds, it is important to know how to make the most of it and earn most of it. Estimation is an essential key, and you may have done this in the past when you attempt to price an item before you go to the grocery to know how much money to withdraw for your needs. The same skill applies here, and with the cost estimations provided in the previous chapter, you can predict how much you will need each day for your food truck to operate.

- **Food and Labor Cost Prediction**

Let's start with labor costs because this is more or less a refresher course at this point in the book. Labor costs are dependent on the number of employees you have, plus the number of shifts that they serve, multiplied by the prevailing wage in your area to comply with labor regulations for your locale. You need to factor in how much of a payroll tax needs to be applied from the product you have obtained (which takes at least 10-12 percent of your labor costs). Not everybody can be paid at the same rate because, remember, your employees' wages are dependent on their experience and abilities.

Food costs are a little hard to predict because the price of food changes in accordance with their value on the market. There is also the seasonality of the farm produce that is involved with the production of food. How does this work? If you are a vegetarian food truck, chances are you are heavily dependent on produce. Spring vegetables such as peas are in high production and are therefore cheaper in the spring months. Squash and beans, which are summer vegetables, are more expensive in the fall and winter months because they are out of season. This is why it is important to consider seasonality in your food truck's operation and your food costs' estimation.

The price of the raw ingredients, the prep work that goes into them, and the use of fuel and electricity, all factor in how much food should actually cost. Like the labor costs, there is a formula to be followed with the computation of the food costs:

Cost of Goods Sold (COGS) / Sales Generated from the Specific Item Made from the Goods

Separated, this means:

(Beginning Inventory + Purchases – Ending Inventory) / Sales Generated from the Item

To determine the cost of goods sold, take note of the items enclosed in the parentheses, as with standard math operations, before you divide the difference with the number of sales generated from the food item it comprises.

If you will recall, in the previous chapter, the Cost of Goods Sold was defined as the number of goods spent to make a specific dish. Thus, if your dish has numerous elements to it, it can be more costly. The computation of food costs will be beneficial because it helps you determine which items on the menu are the most profitable (and therefore, should be mainstays) and the least profitable (which indicates a change in that menu item).

The identification of the costs of goods sold is best calculated through your inventory when you can determine the price you paid for each ingredient that went into a dish. Obtain the sum from the price of the items that make up the dish.

Additional formulae to be taken into consideration include computations for the food cost per item and the total sales per item. For this specific section, we will tackle the food cost per item, which has the formula:

Food Cost of Ingredients X Amount Sold Per Week Average Sales
The computation of average sales requires a different formula, and this is used to determine the ideal food cost

percentage. The formula for the computation of the total sales per dish is:

Total Cost per Dish / Total Sales Per Dish

From here, you would be able to discern with accuracy which dishes on your menu are a hit and which need to be changed for something else or cut off from the menu entirely. From the total sales per dish and the total cost per dish, it is now possible to compute the ideal food cost percentage, which determines how profitable your food truck can be.

The optimum food cost percentage is calculated as follows:

Total Cost per Dish / Total Sales Per Dish

To determine food costs, the ideal percentage for food costs is approximately 25% of your costs. A more conservative estimate places food costs at approximately 30%, with an additional 5% added to account for food wastage or spoilage. The actual food cost, to make for a profitable food truck, should match or be below the ideal food cost.

The 30% of the food costs plus 30% of the labor costs would help determine how much your food truck can make in a single day.

How Can You Optimize Food Costs?

- Flexibility in the menu prices is ideal, and any increases that need to be made with the prices on the menu need to be done in smaller increments.

- Because you can now identify which dishes are the most and least profitable, construct your menu around the more profitable items. If your concept involves a new daily special, consider making the more profitable dish a mainstay.

- As products such as potatoes and pasta are cheaper to purchase in bulk, fill up on carbs.

- Menu design matters as it highlights the dishes that are crowd-pleasers and suggests other items that the customer may want to consider trying from your food truck.

- Take a look around other food suppliers, and do not buy immediately from the first commissary you arrive at. Chances are, you can get the same quality of ingredients somewhere else at a lower rate.

- Pay attention to portion size, as this is where consistency in how food is prepared and served comes in. Equal portion sizes ensure consistency in service and that no one receives too much or too little of an element on a dish. If a dish is too heavy, for instance, reduce the portion size.

- Free items are great but exercise moderation. You may want to give a perk with every item, such as a dollar off or a free drink, but if you watch shows like the Great Food Truck Race, you will realize that some perks end up taking their toll on your business with the expenses needed to supply them.

- Seasonality helps you obtain cheaper produce at the right times and help create a menu that would be popular at a specific time. Examples of this were provided earlier in this chapter.

Set a Production Time

Once the ingredients and equipment have been purchased, a second factor to consider is the speed at which food is prepared and sold. We've probably experienced the impatience of waiting for a particular item and requesting a refund of the money paid earlier, and the same concept applies here. The exception is that you are on the receiving end of the potential impatience of customers who do not want to wait long for your food truck to open and for your food truck to prepare, serve, and sell your food.

Aside from this, a set production time increases the efficiency and productivity at which you and your employees operate the food truck. This is visible through how quickly a dish on the menu comes together and is sold to the customer. Even the simplest dishes require a certain amount of preparation work, so it is important to be prepared beforehand.

The layout of the food truck plays a significant role in how you can streamline the preparation of food, and this will be discussed later on. What is important now is how fast can a particular food be prepared and sold. If you are a chef, you know the importance of **mise en place,** and the same can be applied here. Suggested approaches, but the one that works best would be that of an assembly line, where one person is in charge of a specific element; that way, all parts of the dish are prepared, then assembled for rapid output.

Estimate Commissary Costs

We still have not completely covered the importance of estimation of food costs in the food truck industry, and earlier on, the Cost of Goods Sold remained an important part to determine the potential earning capacity of the food truck.

A commissary, in this instance, according to the definition provided by Florida Law, refers to an establishment that is meant to provide support to the food truck. This form of support can vary and ranges from the provision of potable water (always a necessity in the food truck), the storage of food ingredients, and, if needed, a place that can serve as a site to prep the food for your food truck. This differs from a depot, which is a storage facility where the food truck can stay overnight, which in turn could also add to your costs.

Before we delve into the estimation of how much is needed to pay a commissary, it is important to note that if you live in an urbanized area, such as the large cities, with an established food truck industry, it would be best if you take a look around at the other commissaries, so that you have an overview of the prices. This may not be the case with smaller cities, and you may have to work with what you have. Specialty restaurants such as brunch restaurants and culinary schools are a good place to start in lieu of a commissary.

Before you begin cost estimation, there are two alternatives to choose from: rent a commissary or build one. Again, the latter may be an option if you have the cash to spare as this is likely to be more expensive than your food truck costs, which makes the rental of a commissary the more viable option.

The commissary costs are categorized as "sunk" costs, which means that the expense is already paid for regardless of what happens. While it might be tempting to find a workaround, this is not a good idea. Most laws require food trucks to operate out of a commissary, which would depend on your city's laws. Without a commissary, chances are you will NOT be allowed to operate, which is why there is the need for alternatives.

In Chicago, for example, all preparatory work for the food truck must be done at the commissary, then assembled there – which makes sense considering that your supplies are also stored there. If you do have one, this must be supported by paperwork. The term varies from city to city, which ranges from proof of commissary or the affidavit of commissary, but we will expatiate more on this later.

There is no formula for the computation of commissary costs, which is why you need to check out the ones in your area to identify the more reasonable price or another alternative that can work. The expenses are straightforward, with estimated costs to range from approximately $400 a month to as much as $1200 a month, though this may vary.

The commissary is an essential part of the food truck industry, and without it, your food truck cannot operate, so it is an unavoidable cost, much like rent and insurance payments. It is important to take commissary costs into account when identifying the profitability of the food truck.

Volume Generation

This section refers to the economic context of volume, not the one on your remote control. Simply put, volume is the number of customers you can obtain while the food truck operates, which is important as a high volume means more customers, in return, more income. It is important now that you and your employees can keep up with the crowd's demands and ensure that everyone is satisfied with your services.

This is a concept best utilized if you are planning to expand your food truck. If this is not in your immediate plans, you will want to read ahead. Another context where volume generation can be applied would be the purchase of food items. If you do choose to expand and serve more customers, you can ultimately drive your food costs lower as you can avail of discounts given with bulk purchases and discounts for the use of the commercial kitchens (if you use one).

Back to the customers, there are various means by which you can drum up business, but this will be elaborated on in later chapters. In Chapter 1, it was mentioned that one of the traits needed is to sell yourself, and it was stated that you are selling your idea to customers. Let's face it: if consumers enjoy the concept, they will return.

X Marks the Spot: Location is Everything

As it says in this chapter, location is one of the main determinants of the success of your food truck, where the smallest of details can affect the number of sales that your food truck can generate. Again, research makes a reappearance, although if you did your industry analysis earlier when you were creating your business plan, there is a high chance that you will be able to identify the areas that are more likely to have a reasonable amount of pedestrian traffic – the lifeblood of the food truck industry.

When you do your research, consider and visualize where you want your food truck to be located. How do you want your food truck to be placed in the specific area you want? How visible do you want your food truck to be? Other things to consider are the space you want to occupy, and can you fit your food truck in there? Does your food truck operate in a location that expresses something about your business? This may be difficult to understand at first, but consider it from the perspective of whether or not my food truck will interest the folks that frequent this location. With a question of visibility, think, can my food truck be seen by customers when they walk down the sidewalk?

Social media will be extremely useful in this case, as this would help you identify events in the area that you can use to your advantage and generate more sales. Additionally, keep an eye out for other places with heavy foot traffic, such as malls, theaters, and stadiums. Bus and train stations would also be good places to set up your food truck. You cannot go wrong with college campuses as food truck sites.

When you determine the location of your food truck, it is important to get the lay of the land for yourself. Read the people, and take note of their behaviors in that area. If you choose a spot in a park that is near a residential area, for example, the residents of the nearby houses could be out jogging in the park or walking the dog, and this is your chance to observe. For another example, if you choose a commercial area, you want to make friends with the doormen and security guards. Why? Because they are in the position to observe the streets and the people and most likely know where the best spots to park in the city are. Aside from the visibility and placement of your food truck, there are several conveniences that have to be placed in mind: Comfort Rooms, ATMs, and Banks. Why these three, you may ask?

- Let's start with Comfort Rooms; for the most obvious reason, you cannot afford to be short-handed in the food truck just because an employee took a really long bathroom break simply because there is no convenient bathroom. A nearby comfort room would help shorten bathroom breaks and improve the productivity of your food truck.

- Second, ATMs. One of the items mentioned as part of the start-up costs included the use of a credit-card reader, which would help increase the number of transactions that you can take in your food truck. Remember, it is important to be prepared for eventualities in this industry. One of these eventualities is the lack of a credit-card reader because you did not purchase one, or if you did purchase one, it glitched out. Regardless, ATMs come in handy as a ready source for cash if your customers encounter this problem.

- Lastly, Banks, not for a loan, but as a ready source for change, for customers who pay with large bills, and if you need coins.

Once you have the location, an important part of increasing the volume of customers would be to engage with them. One of the joys of the food truck business is your ability to move quickly; thus, it would be important to take note of prime locations that you encounter in your route. Most importantly, seize the opportunity when it presents itself; you never know when you just land in a prime selling area because of serendipity.

Though you may have done the research for the needed analyses that form part of your business plan, you will need to do more in-depth research into several planned locations. Several, so you have a back-up plan in case other spots you have eyed are unavailable or do not permit the operation of food trucks. Think of this as less research and more of a reconnaissance mission to know the best times to visit a certain location and the worst times to set up shop in the same area. This is also the time that you begin to take note of how many people visit the sites you have planned and the traffic – a frequent problem, especially in urbanized areas.

3.1 Predict the Smoothest Route to Foot Traffic Hotspots

Because opening the actual food truck takes time, with all the prep work, take note of two specific time periods for the location you have chosen: the time you have chosen to set up and the time you have noted to be rush hour. An essential skill now is to know the parking situation in your chosen location, if there are any potential snags that you will encounter. If you encounter this difficulty, plan for an earlier start to ensure that you retain that spot that you wanted.

Your research, after all this, should contain the subsequent information in the form of a map for the sake of convenience: The other stores and their products, a contact list of other businesses (this may come in handy especially if you are flooded with customers and are unable to purchase supplies yourself, this list includes services that can deliver supplies to your location (a really great convenience), other street vendors (you never know when you can collaborate), the bank, restrooms, parking rules in the area, and the best parking areas for your food truck listed in priority.

The initiation of sales involves the creation of relationships; thus, on the first day of operations in that location, take note to visit the spot early. If someone took your spot, rein in that impatience and use a few strategies to net the same area.

- Wait for the spot to open up, especially if it's a delivery van (they don't often linger) or if it is a person with an errand. Patience will pay off once you have secured your favored parking spot.
- Parking meters. Keep an eye on them, and make sure that you feed the meter with the needed change to ensure you do not get fined for parking next to an expired meter.
- Be nice to other drivers; you can switch spots if the driver feels you do not get enough exposure in your chosen area.
- If the vehicle is a commercial one, more likely, there is a number that can be called. Politely explain your situation and ask if it is possible to swap parking spaces. You never know, the great parking opportunity is just a phone call away.

Cleanliness matters in the parking area, so no matter how messy the area was before, clean-up remains a priority. Pick up the mess, dispose of it, and begin the rounds to sell your food, or let the presence of your food truck be felt to begin to drum up the foot traffic that you need. Invite people, and If there are any hostile vendors, treat them nicely but subtly let them know that you are not backing down.

Lastly, with consideration to the location of the food truck, there is also the time that you plan to start your operations in the said location. The best-laid plans often do not work out In your favor, so if you plan to open by a certain time, you will want to open a month ahead just to iron out all the wrinkles in how your food truck operates. This will ensure that your food truck can operate at optimal capacity by the time you are officially opened and ready for the selling season.

3.2 Efficient Food Production

We talked about the food preparation that needs to be done at the commissary and the use of the mise en place with food preparation to facilitate the ease at which food is assembled once at the food truck. To be efficient, food production must take into consideration what goes into your meals, and therefore, dishes that can be produced, assembled, and served quickly are essential to food truck success, as well as to its profitability.

- **Consistency Is Key**

  Your food truck is your idea, and it is important that for it to be successful, the identity of your food truck's idea is preserved with the production and sale of consistent dishes. The experience that drew customers to your food truck should be experienced by them every time they approach and purchase from your food truck., the fast-food industry is what it is because of consistent products, and this is what your food truck can be too because it helps your customers know that your product is known for making superior quality food items. Customers expect a certain quality of food from your food truck, and returning customers certainly expect the same quality they had in their first visit. This is central to the success of your food truck.

  How can this be done? There are several forms of consistency that need to be maintained aside from the quality of your food. These include the service you give to customers, the identity you convey through your brand and food, and how you treat everyone around you – your customers, employees, and suppliers. Consistency can be maintained with a few strategic moves.

Strategies to Ensure Consistent Quality of Food Items

- Food recipes that your staff can prepare should be clearly and easily understood and have clear specifications about how much of an item should be on the dish. It might be helpful to create a list and work with weights such as grams to ensure that portion size remains consistent as well.

- Take the time to train your staff (this will be elaborated on later in the book) and how you expect each menu item to taste and look. Give them samples and teach them how to prepare the said menu item.

- Appraise your team about the items and other necessary tasks that need to be done daily in the food truck. This includes the prep work, storage of the perishables, cleanliness of the truck, maintenance (especially gas and power), paperwork, and even the attitudes they adapt when dealing with customers.
- Aside from this, do not be lenient with the quality of your food. This is your identity, your food, your idea, and you do not want anything or anyone to tarnish your idea that made the food truck in the first place.

The idea of consistency is as:

-important as the price for your food truck,

-relevant to the attractiveness of the food truck as that is.

As a result, you must maintain the same level of excellence throughout the year regardless of whether you're operating your food truck during the day or at night.

3.3   Straighten out the Staff: Why Hiring the Right People Matters

As much as the food truck relies on the food alone, you also need to depend on the right people to man your food truck. If you are a part of the crew of the food truck, that's great, it's a hands-on approach for you and the two others in your food truck. First off, two others? Remember, the food truck's kitchen is a limited space, and you have to contend with the cramped spaces. It is a bit of a stretch to have more than three people at a time in the same space.

Before you start searching for your employees, you will need the necessary paperwork to ensure that you can legally hire employees and have a prepared set of rules, guidelines, and forms that you can give to your new hires if they meet your approval. Your preparedness for this step shows to the potential employee that you are serious in your desire to operate a food truck, and they, in turn, will take your business seriously and follow your guidelines.

Where to Look?

While it may be tempting to post a help wanted ad In your local newspaper, you will want to check with other food truck owners and restaurants about where they were able to find their staff. Chances are there are employment agencies out there who cater to employers in the food industry and have a ready pool of qualified employees to choose from.

You do need to be clear about the job description of the specific role before you even make your job post, and keep this on file in the event that you need to use or consult it. Provide as much information as possible on the role that you need your employee to fill, including the shifts if need be. The information you provide ensures transparency with your employees regarding what you expect from them while the food truck operates. Detail the potential difficulties that they may encounter as your employees.

What to Look For in an Employee?

It is not enough that you are able to find employees, as some skills can be taught to them as you train your employees, provided they have the motivation to learn new skills. However, there are certain qualifications that mere training will not cover, especially if the employee does not know how to drive. Because of this, when you create your job post in your search for employees, if you need your employees to know how to drive, indicate this on the post.

Apart from the skill in driving, employees need to be committed to working in all seasons, not leave you short-handed when it gets uncomfortable working in the food truck. Food trucks, despite their construction, still get uncomfortably hot in summer and equally cold in winter, so your employees should have the fortitude to get through these times.

If your food truck is a seasonal enterprise, indicate this when you post for a job and interview potential employees, so they will not be disappointed in your business as well. Provide incentives for your employees to commit throughout these times.

Aside from the fortitude of your employees as well as their ability to drive, there are other skills that your employees must have to make your food truck operate efficiently. These include the ability to exude energy in the way that they act and carry themselves (You can often gain an impression of this in an interview), do they take pride in what they do and honest about their past experiences (this is indicative of the integrity of an employee and it is always a good quality in an employee). If the employee is curious as to the operation of the business and their role in your business, then curiosity equates to intelligence and the need to learn (this is also indicative of their motivation), and if the employee is mature in the way that they take on responsibilities and are respectful of ALL customers (this is also among the qualities of a great sale person).

What to Ask an Interviewee?

It can be easy to ask the interviewee about themselves; however, in business, there is a certain degree of probity that needs to be exercised to ensure that your business only takes on the best employees there are. Avoid theoretical questions – these can easily be expounded on and not give a true indication of the actual abilities and demeanor of an interviewee. Instead, focus on the subsequent topics and add in accordance with your discretion.

- Job experience (What they liked or disliked about their most recent job and why they left)
- Experience with food (what is the best food memory they have had)
- Motivation (Why a food truck than, say, a restaurant or café?)
- Ideals (What do they think makes a good employee for a food truck?)
- Customer Service Experience (How did they deal with good or bad customers in the past?)

This is not a set formula, as you would have to ask follow-up questions according to the interviewee's responses. If you have a friend with HR experience, consult with them to enhance the interview questions. Aside from the interviewee, consult their references sheet and conduct another set of interviews on your own. Learn more about the employee from their past employers and ask about how the employee was in their business and what made the employee work best there. Learn about the strengths of the employee as well as the weaknesses.

Once you have determined the crew for your food truck, the next step involves the training sessions to ensure that they familiarize themselves with the concept of your food truck, as well as the preparation of food, how it should be served, the maintenance of the truck and other topics as you may see fit. To save effort on your part, ideally, training sessions should be conducted with the entire group regardless of what shift they will serve. This is more economical and encourages the team to interact and form relationships with each other and your business.

3.4   Conclusion

The first three chapters of this book are designed to introduce you to the food truck industry from the perspective of the business owner. Far from the simple setup that you would envision, the food truck business involves a wholehearted commitment and dedication to ensure that it remains a viable business. There are several concepts that you can adopt; however, at the core of it all is the desire to provide readily available food with speedy service through customers. Because of this, it is important that you establish a plan to ensure that the set-up of your food truck is as smooth as possible.

There is no secret formula that guarantees the immediate profitability of your business. It all boils down to how hard you work as the food truck entrepreneur and your will to succeed. Consistency in service and quality paired with the right people at the food truck with your training and preparation are the main ingredients to be successful in your food truck.

BOOK 2: Setting Up Your Food Truck Business: Legalities, Setting Up Your Food Truck, Testing phase, Buyer Persona Analysis and Branding

4 The Legalities of the Food Truck

As it has been discussed in book 1 of this series, the food truck industry is an industry that requires a lot of commitment and hard work. Book 1 has introduced us to the business enviro and how to start the business from scratch from the business owner's perspective. The next step in the food truck business would be to prepare for the legalities to own a food truck, and in this chapter, you will be apprised of the licenses and permits that you will need before your food truck can operate. Depending on your location, regulations that concern the operation of the food truck may vary from state to state or country to country. It would be best to do some research on the specifics. Properly prepared paperwork can ultimately save you on potential costs from fines and penalties that the relevant authorities can impose.

As a food truck owner, you have a lot to deal with, which is why there is the need for professionals to consult concerning taxes and the other legalities that can ensue once your business commences. There are three professionals whose help you will need before you move forward: an accountant, a lawyer, and an insurance provider, as most permits to operate concern these three professionals.

4.1 Untangle the Legalities Before Going on the Road

The best way to avoid any legal troubles with the operation of your food truck is to prevent them. This requires the help of an attorney. If you happen to have one on call, that would be great. If you do not, there are several sites to help you find an attorney who can help you with the legalities that can arise from the food truck operation. Why would you need an attorney in the first place?

- Attorneys-at-Law can anticipate potential legal troubles as you operate your food truck and save you on costs from liabilities that may arise as your food truck operates.

- Attorneys-at-Law can identify the regulations that you may have overlooked and help you rectify them, which saves you from the penalties that the relevant authorities can impose.
- Employment records and applications are double-checked by your attorney to ensure that your questions are not discriminatory and can draft the agreements needed between you and your employees. Additionally, if you have imposed any rules and regulations, the attorney can ensure that these are in compliance with existent labor laws applicable to your state or country.

While it would be a great idea to just make an appointment with your nearest attorney, an ideal attorney would have to be familiar with the intricacies of the food truck industry. Therefore, it would be a good idea to consult with other food truck owners to see who they have on retainer, as this would save you time on an attorney who knows what needs to be done for your food truck business.

If this is not possible, attorney listing sites such as www.lawyerlegion.com and www.martindale.com are great sites to begin your search for an experienced attorney in your area. Use filters to narrow down attorneys according to your needs and preferences. Once you have chosen your attorney, carefully read the fine print with regards to the fees and negotiate with the fee structure and costs that are best for your business. Finally, don't be afraid to ask for references; think of it as another form of an interview process to learn how your attorney works for other people.

It is important that you obtain competent legal counsel to ensure that you are well represented in the event that legal troubles arise. If your lawyer does not get back to you for a length of time, consider a different lawyer to cut down on costs.

Accountants are the next necessity for legal tangles related to the taxes incurred as you operate your food truck. Accountants are familiar with business models and can advise you on the best option to utilize for your food truck business and how this affects the taxes that will be imposed. The presence of an accountant will help bolster the credibility of your business plan if you plan to approach a bank for a loan, with the additional perk of the advice to be gained as you determine the right loan option for your plans.

Additionally, accountants are able to help you analyze your finances and help you determine any changes that are to be made. If you recall cost estimation in the previous chapter, accountants can help you determine which items are selling the least, so you can make the adjustments needed to your menu and how you manage your inventory to save on costs. Accountants may also find ways to net you exemptions that you are entitled to and lower the amount of taxes you have to pay.

Lastly, accountants can help with the determination of your employees' payroll and the taxes that accompany them. Accountants can give advice on the insurance plans, employees' benefits, and other expenses and responsibilities that you have as a business owner.

As with attorneys, it would be best to have an accountant on retainer who is familiar with the food truck business. Consult with your lawyer or other food truck owners to see which accountant they use for their record keeping. A CPA would have the qualifications that you will seek and is equipped to deal with the IRS. A general accountant would do for simple tasks such as tax returns and bookkeeping.

Insurance Providers are an absolute necessity in the food truck business. There are several types of insurance that you will need for your business: the standard liability insurance; for your employees, you will need workers' compensation; and complete coverage for the food truck itself. Ideally, the insurance provider should provide you with the insurance coverage ideal for your business needs and reduce the risks to your food truck, all at a cost that will not strain your finances.

Other food truck owners can recommend a good insurance provider who has experience with the food truck industry. There are also insurance providers who specialize in this industry, such as www.insureon.com/food-business-insurance/food-trucks and www.progressivecommercial.com/business-insurance/professions/food-truck-insurance/ to name a few. You will need to check if they can operate in your state and if these insurance providers have a good reputation in the business.

Insurance providers can be agents or brokers. Use an **agent** if you only have one food truck with few employees. Insurance agents are employed by an insurance carrier, and thus, you would save on costs as you are not charged additional fees for their services. Speak with several agents to find one with the coverage that your food truck will need. Use a **broker** if you have more than one food truck or numerous employees. Brokers sell for several insurance companies and are paid by commission, which can increase your insurance costs.

You can be the main contact with the insurance provider, or if your business is large enough, let a manager be the one to handle the insurance issues to avoid confusion.

4.2   Business Structures

Several options are available to you as a business owner regarding how your food truck is run. For example, a food truck can be run as part of a single proprietorship, a partnership, or as part of a corporation (especially if you are a food truck franchisee), which can affect the legalities of the food truck business. Below is an overview of the usual business structures that are to be found in the food truck industry.

- **Sole Proprietorship** refers to a business structure where it is owned by a single person. Legally, there is no distinction made between a business in sole proprietorship and your food truck business, which enables you to keep what you make with the applicable taxes to be deducted from your income. The main disadvantage with this type of structure is that if there are disputes –legal, financial, etc.– while running the business, your personal property may be forfeited to settle the terms of the dispute. In the business, you may operate under your name or the name of your food truck due to the lack of legal distinction, and you can hire any number of employees as you are not considered an employee in the eyes of the law.
- **Partnerships** are an unincorporated business structure that comes in two types: General and Limited Partnerships. Both types of partnerships have a shared disadvantage in that because

this partnership is not incorporated, personal liability for debts and obligations is carried by the partnership.

- o Partnerships can be made with close friends; however, because business is involved, there are certain tangles that need to be ironed out between you and your friends, and this is best done with the help of legal counsel for each member of the partnership. Common concerns include:
    - Ownership, to determine how much a stake the partners have in the business, as the partners are able to contribute resources to help keep the business afloat. This is considered their investment into the business, which calls for their stake in the ownership of the business.
    - Distribution of Gains and Losses to know how these should be divided among the partners. This includes any other compensation for the partners, if there are any.
    - Responsibilities, though this may not apply to limited partners. Each member of the partnership must be provided with their respective roles and responsibilities and who makes the decisions with regards to concerns on food truck operations.
    - Termination of Partnership, as one should be prepared in the event that the partner chooses to sell their stake in the business or their share is bought out by another partner, or simply the partner is incapacitated in some form.
- o This is best consolidated with the help of legal counsel to account for all theoretical possibilities that the partnership may encounter to prevent any legal tangles and hinder the operation of the food truck.
- o **General Partnerships** consist of two or more partners who take part in the business and manage the debts and

operations of the food truck. Both partners contribute various resources towards the business, and they both profit equally from the business and share in any losses. The main advantage of this type of business structure is that businesses classified under this are exempt from income tax. Any profits or losses are coursed through all the members of the partnership.

- o **Limited Partnerships** can include the general partners and limited partners who function as the investors of the business who do NOT share the same liabilities as with the general partners of the business. Because Limited Partners tend to be quiet partners, you have more influence in how the company is managed with a limited partnership.

- **Corporations** are formed when one incorporates a business under the terms provided for by Corporate Law. Corporations are usually businesses but can also be charities and government entities, for example. A company is legally defined as a legal body, and the law classifies it as having the capacity to file lawsuits and establish contracts. Corporations may belong solely to one person, though this will depend on the corporation's rules in your country. A main advantage with the corporation is that by virtue of its legal personality, the debts incurred by the corporation remain separate from your personal liabilities,

  - o For the food truck business, incorporation would create several benefits, which include protection from personal liability as the corporation is counted as a legal person with its personality. Therefore, in the event of a suit, only assets of the corporation, not your personal assets, may be the subject of compensation.

  - o Tax benefits are there; however, in accordance with your state or country's laws, you will want to consult with your accountant to determine the benefits that could be attained if a business is incorporated.

o   When you need more funds to expand your food truck idea, this task is made easy by selling stocks in the corporation.

Disadvantages of a Corporation

- Paperwork, although if you have an accountant, this should not be much of an issue. Corporations are their own entity and have separate obligations to the government. You, as a person, also have the same obligations under the taxation power of the government. It would be important to organize your records to ensure that no confusion arises.
- Costs are determinant by your area and local corporation code. There are minimum requirements that may be set to establish a corporation, and this may include the amount of money invested, which may form part of the articles of incorporation; hence, it can increase the costs needed to open the food truck.

The state government or your country's government must be made aware of the presence of your corporation. Before you choose to incorporate your business, be sure to consult with your lawyer to ensure that this is the best option for your business.

4.3   Limitations of the Food Truck

This section does not deal precisely with the limitations of how your food truck operates; instead, it deals with the regulations that you need to be aware of before you begin selling food from your truck. Food truck regulations are quite strict as you have to contend with the business, mobile restaurant, and vehicle regulations. Each of these regulations must be followed in accordance with your local laws. This is where your attorney comes in because aside from these regulations, there are several more categories of laws that you would come into contact with as the food truck owner.

- The laws that pertain to how your **business structure** has been given a brief overview in the previous section.
- **Consumer Protection Laws** prevent the abuse of customers through unfair business practices as well as from fraud.
- **Employment Laws**, which will be elaborated on later, relate to the wages, benefits, and protections that are afforded by the laws for your employees. You may be included under its jurisdiction, provided you are considered an employee by the definition of your country's labor laws. When unsure of the terminology or the interpretation, please consult with your lawyer.
    - For those in the United States, a great resource to get started on these laws can be found at www.dol.gov/agencies/whd/state
    - For those in the United Kingdom, visit www.iclg.com/practice-areas/employment-and-labour-laws-and-regulations/united-kingdom
    - Canadian laws may vary from province to province, www.canada.ca/en/services/jobs/workplace/federal-labour-standards.html is a good place to start.
    - Indian Labor Laws may find their resources at www.iclg.com/practice-areas/employment-and-labour-laws-and-regulations/india
- **Environmental Laws** ensure that your business remains compliant with the environmental regulations of your specific area. The main concern for these laws is the disposal of any hazardous material that your food truck may produce. As such, some research will need to be done to include provisions for this in your food truck.
- **Taxation Laws,** which in itself is one of the powers of the Government, are best discussed with your Lawyer and your Accountant, as these can cover Income Taxes, Sales Taxes, and other applicable taxes, which will be elaborated on in the next section.

- Because the food truck and its brand are your ideas, another law that applies to your food truck would be **Intellectual Property Laws,** which include the Trademark and Patent of your Brand and the Brand Names. This ensures that no other food trucks out there have the same name and have the same food.
- Lastly, since your food truck is mobile and can sell and occupy various spaces, Zoning Laws ensure that your food truck operates in an area permitted by your city.

4.4   Licenses, Permits, and Taxes

To understand this chapter in its legal application, it would be best to define what are licenses and permits before we delve into their variations:

- A **license** is a legal document granted by a government authority to exercise a certain privilege that would be impermissible in its nature without the granted authorization. This term is also used to refer to the documentation that confers the permission for the licensee to engage in the conduct prescribed by the permission.
- A **permit** can be interchanged with a license, although, legally, they may not be the same. A permit, in legal channels, is of a temporary nature, though this may vary in accordance with local laws. This is regulatory in nature, and in the context of the food truck, it applies to safety. A permit is granted not upon application but upon the inspection of the place where the permit is to apply.

The license and permit, as well as the requirements needed to fulfill them, will vary from location to location, so it would be a good idea to conduct a few phone calls or visits to ensure that you have prepared the necessary paperwork for the licenses, as well as the necessary adjustments in your food truck for the permits. Business licenses obtained from your area will require the payment of a fee, inquire at your City or Municipal Hall for further details.

4.5 Permits from the Relevant Authorities

Permits ensure regulatory practices, and as mentioned earlier, relate to the safety of the customers and the employees as the food truck operates. This ensures that every aspect of the food truck is up to code according to the prescribed criteria created by your local laws.

- **The Food Handler's Permit** may be required by local, municipal, and state laws for your employees. More often, attendance at a food safety class for a specific number of hours is required before this permit can be issued. This seminar is conducted by the local health and safety authorities. This is a requirement that you should strictly enforce with your employees, especially when the truck operates.

- **Health Department Permits** are provided upon the inspection of your food truck and commissary by the health department to ensure that the place where food preparation takes place and where food assemblage takes place is up to the standards prescribed by the health department.

- **Fire Certificates** are essential, especially if your food truck contains cooking equipment and utilizes fuels, such as propane, as the source of energy. Fire Certificates are issued by your local fire department and may require you or an employee to attend a Safety Course on how to deal with fires. The Safety Course will also apprise you concerning the regulations you need to follow and what your food truck must comply with. In addition, routine inspections are to be expected, so it is important that the fire suppression mechanisms of the food truck are up to code.

- To gain full authorization to sell your food items, some areas may require you to obtain a **Seller's Permit.** An advantage of the seller's permit is that you can purchase items at wholesale prices without the accompanying sales tax.

In certain cases, special training is required, but this is essential for your food truck to be in operation.

Licenses for Food, Liquor, and Music

Going back to the legal definition of a license, it refers to the authorization given to you by a governmental authority to perform an act that would otherwise be prohibited by law. This is made apparent with the presence of the needed licenses – the permission granted to you in paper form – to ensure that your food truck has the necessary permission to perform the acts that it intends to do.

- Because foremost the food truck is a mobile vehicle, an important requisite for the food truck and its employees is that the person who drives it has a valid **Driver's License** that is issued by the State Authorities or the Government Authority in accordance with your specific locale. The type of driver's license may vary with the size of your food truck, as larger trucks may require a different type of license altogether, just to prove that you know how to drive a commercial food truck.

- The food truck itself requires a **Vehicle's License** and the registrations needed for it to be able to drive all over the specific place.

- Before you operate, a **Business License** must be obtained from the local or municipal hall. Fees for this type of license may vary, so consult with your town hall. This can be part of the gross total sales or a yearly sum that must be paid to be able to renew your business license.

- A **music license** is an optional license, especially if you don't plan to use music as a means to attract customers. However, it is important for food trucks with jingles as part of their gimmick to attract customers as zoning laws and local ordinances may prohibit loud music from being played in specific areas.

- A **liquor license** is a relative rarity among food trucks, especially if your food truck does not sell liquor. This is optional, but if you intend to sell alcoholic beverages with your food, it is necessary. Some areas may not permit the distribution of alcohol through a food truck. It would be best to consult with your local authorities to see if such a permit can be issued to your food truck.

- Additional requirements may include a **Facility Record**; this means the proof of a commissary and has been discussed earlier. It may be forbidden by law to prep food in a food truck, which is why a commissary is needed as a measure to ensure that you have a safe place where you can prepare your food truck menu, as well as a place where you can dispose of your waste.
- A novel addition for cities that have regulated the food truck industry would be the **mobile food truck license** – which could entail that there are only a limited amount of food trucks that can operate in the city. In which case, you would need to prepare all the requisite paperwork to ensure you can obtain these.

These licenses and permits are a necessary step to ensure that your food truck is properly documented and has the needed permission to operate. Continuously updated paperwork for the food truck is essential to prevent a halt in operations, potentially hindering the number of sales that your food truck can make. Updated paperwork also means a lower chance of penalties imposed by the relevant issuing authorities and more savings on costs for your business.

4.6   Prerequisites before Hiring Staff

We've spoken about the characteristics you should be seeking when hiring new employees. Even if you've never driven before, you should acquire a driver's license and a food handler's permit anyway. However, there are certain legalities that are provided for in your local labor laws – you can view the links provided in the section on employment laws. The IRS requires you to get an Employer Identification Number (EIN) for your company, a nine-digit number comparable to a Social Security Number. An entity must register with both the state and federal governments if it does business in the state. Obtain an EIN with an application through this website **www.irs.gov/Businesses/Small-Businesses-&-Self-Employed/Apply-for-an-Employer-Identification-Number-(EIN)-Online.** Once you have an EIN issued to you and your business has been registered, you can commence with hiring employees.

Each state may issue its own EIN, so it is important to check with your state's labor practices. If you are in Canada, the UK, or India, you will want to check the respective requirements set forth by your ministries in the links under Employment Laws.

There are several forms that your employees must fill out before they can be hired. These forms have to do with tax forms that are required by the IRS.

- The **Form W-4** contains information on how much federal income tax must be deducted from the employee's earnings. In order to avoid a fine, please send this form to the IRS.

- You, as an employer, must complete the **W-2 form**. The coverage includes tax withholdings from workers' salaries and paychecks for the entire year for tax statements. This must be sent to your workers by January 31 and outlines your previous year's profits and taxes. You must mail a copy of Form W-2 before the end of February or by the end of the last business day of February.

- **State Tax Forms** carry no specific code, but their tax requirements may vary. Check out your state's requirements and forms through this website http://www.bls.gov/jobs to learn more about what you need.

To ensure that your employment taxes are properly filed, keep a record of your employment taxes for at least six years so you can easily accomplish the needed forms required by the IRS for your taxes.

If you hire foreign employees to work for your food truck, additional paperwork is needed to determine their eligibility.

- **Form I-9, Section 1** contains relevant information such as the employee's contact information and their Social Security Number and Employment Eligibility.
- A Valid ID with the supportive documentation from a prescribed list by the Federal Government must be presented to

you by the third day of Enrollment. These lists can be seen through these sites:

- o One ID from List A: www.uscis.gov/i-9-central/acceptable-documents/list-documents/form-i-9-acceptable-documents
- o Or, one ID from each of the two lists B and C: www.uscis.gov/i-9-central/acceptable-documents/list-documents/form-i-9-acceptable-documents?topic_id=1&t=b
- o www.uscis.gov/i-9-central/acceptable-documents/list-documents/form-i-9-acceptable-documents?topic_id=1&t=c

- This is usually enough to verify foreign workers; however, enrolment in the E-Verify Program may be needed through this site. www.uscis.gov/e-verify
- Keep form I-9 with you on file for three years as this is not sent to the federal government, or keep it with you for a year after the employee leaves your service.

Once you have hired an employee, additional federal requirements include the subsequent steps:

- New and rehired employees must be reported to your state's respective Labor Agency. Additional requirements can be viewed through the Small Business Administration's website at www.sba.gov/content/new-hire-reporting-your-state.
- There is the matter of worker's compensation insurance, necessary if a worker becomes ill or injured in the course of their work. Identify what are the requirements you need, and determine what are the best compensation plans for your business through this guide provided by the National Federation of Independent Businesses: http://www.nfib.com/article/workers-compensation-laws-state-by-state-comparison-57181/
- Payroll methods are at your discretion or through the use of a payroll service. Most payroll services have the added convenience of dealing with the SBA Requirements on the

Reporting of New Hires and Rehires and the purchase of the most ideal insurance plan for your business and the computation and remittance of the payroll and its taxes to the IRS.

- Workplace posters that inform your employees of their rights are required to be posted at your workplace, though you will have to consult with your local SBA to determine if this remains applicable to food trucks. Regardless of the outcome, you can view the requirements for posting the SBA Workplace Posters through this site: www.sba.gov/content/workplace-posters .

4.7 Relevant Liabilities for Your Food Truck

One of the more important concepts in the food truck operation is the need for insurance, of which there are several types that can be availed of. Apart from the more obvious choices, such as vehicular insurance and workers' compensation insurance, there are several more types of insurance that help protect your business from any other liabilities that may arise in the course of your food truck's operation.

Earlier in this chapter, we discussed how you could find the best insurance provider for your business. To answer this, consider whether or not the insurance plan you are viewing can cover vehicular accidents; if it can cover a food truck; can the policy cover customers who claim food poisoning? Damages to the truck through vandalism, or if the truck becomes stolen? Special coverage for specific items?

The right insurance provider would be able to answer your thoughts and determine the best policy that can cover all these. However, you will need to familiarize yourself with the various types of insurance that will be encountered in the business.

- For vehicles that form part of your business operations, **Commercial Auto Liability** is an absolute necessity. This is different from Personal Auto Liability that permits you to use your vehicle as part of the business because these two policies differ according to their terms set and their coverage. Commercial Auto Liability coverage includes an increased upper limit on coverage and enables the coverage of your food truck under the classification of modified trucks. This coverage includes how far in a set radius that your business remains covered in.

- **General Liability** is a policy that offers several types of coverage that you can select from, with the added benefit of augmenting the chosen policies with additional coverage, if needed. General Liability coverage protects the business from claims caused by injury to customers and damage to property, whether if it is yours or someone else's. This also covers your menu items.

- Any additional equipment you may tow behind you as an accompaniment to your food truck business will require **Business Personal Property Liability**, which covers these items such as a smoker or grill, for instance. However, This form of coverage does not cover damages to the said equipment.

- We have discussed **Worker's Compensation Insurance** earlier; for your workers, **Unemployment Insurance** provides compensation for workers who have left your company/business and remain unemployed until such time that they land another job.

- **Umbrella Liability** is the safety blanket that provides additional coverage that goes beyond the coverage provided by the commercial auto liability, general liability, and worker's compensation insurance policies.

Additional coverage may arise from the employee you designate to drive your food truck. This can result in an increase in your instance costs from your auto insurance provider if you have an employee who is considered ineligible. Because of the presence of the ineligible employee, most auto insurance providers will not continue their business which leaves you with the least desirable option of a lesser-known insurance provider with higher insurance costs. To avoid this scenario, it is important that when you screen for your drivers, that as part of the screening process, to have a visit at the Department of Motor Vehicles (or its equivalent in the UK and Canada) and get their Motor Vehicle Reports. Your driver must not have more than three moving violations and no more than two accidents. Additionally, your driver must not have been charged or convicted with offenses such as driving under the influence, having their license suspended, or being convicted of a felony involving cars.

The usual costs of the food truck's coverage as a business owner would cost approximately $105 per month, with an annual cost of $1,260. This is a figure with approximately $1,000,000 in coverage.

Familiarize Your Locale's Regulations

If there is one thing that is constant with the food truck business is that the regulations that govern the industry undergo changes that can affect the way you can operate your food truck; therefore, it is important to the operations and the survival of your business that you are able to remain in the loop for any changes that your local government may impose on the food truck industry.

There are two specific areas that these regulatory processes affect: The design of your food truck with attention to how the interior is laid out and the means you can legally employ to sell food items in your truck. For the regulations that relate to the construction and the layout of the truck, focus is accorded towards the function of the food truck. There are different regulations for trucks that are processing and non-processing. Processing trucks are those trucks where the prep work and assemblage of food are done in the truck. Non-Processing trucks, on the other hand, are trucks that sell pre-made items that have been prepared offsite. Because processing trucks handle food in its raw and unprepared state, there are more regulations that govern it regarding food safety and the competency mandated by health care laws for food workers. However, with trends in the food truck industry in a state of flux, it is entirely possible for regulations to make accommodations for food that has been prepared with the use of more novel techniques.

Truck placement is another element that may be controlled by the food truck. If you've read the preceding chapter, as stated, you should already know the best locations to park your food truck, and you should get good foot traffic in these locations. Additionally, you are acquainted with the limitations and constraints associated with that particular section of your trip. If you happen to have a market as part of your route, a good move would be to identify the local regulations that enable the operation of food establishments near markets. These regulations can take the form of rules on the hours that you are allowed to sell your items or the distance that you have to park away from the market due to prohibitions on the sale of the same or similar products in a particular area.

There are also regulations that limit food trucks to the use of private lots, and in large cities, this may be found alongside food trucks that can sell in the streets. It would be best to be appraised on these regulations to ensure that your food truck does not encounter any obstacles to its operation.

4.8   The Ideal Practices for your Food Truck

It is important to recall that selling food on the street as a food truck owner is a privilege, not a right. If you will recall the section on licenses, where license referred to the permission granted by an authority that enables one to perform an act that would otherwise be illegal were it not for the permission granted. Because of this, it would be imperative that your business follow the regulations that the city has outlined.

- Cleanliness of the area and the use of proper parking practices would be a great start.
- Ensure that you do not block driveways, sidewalks, pedestrian lanes, and fire hydrants.
- Always keep your workstation clean and clear to avoid hazards that can jeopardize the health and safety of your customers.
- After you have finished your sales, ensure that you leave the area clean.

- Pick-up any trash left by your customers and drop them into the nearest trash receptacles.
- Control any noise, especially that of your generator.
- Utilize sustainable environmental practices and avoid the use of Styrofoam-based products and the practice of disposing of used oil down the drain. Go for paper and recyclable products when that option is available.
- Participation in community events would endear you to the community where your route is and ensure that your food truck continually gets patronized. Street fairs and fundraisers for various causes are a great place to cement your food truck's place in your community. This ensures that your food truck becomes a fixture in the community and a steady stream of patrons.
- Not everything is a competition, as your fellow food truck entrepreneurs can be a great source of collaboration and competition. Congregate and collaborate with other food truck owners at the lots or food truck parks. If you specialize in drinks and the other truck specializes in other food items, you do not end up in direct competition with each other. You end up in a synergy that helps increase the number of sales for your respective trucks.
- Call ahead if you intend to join other food trucks in a lot or street, as this is a customary practice to ensure goodwill among your fellow food truck owners. You could learn more information that way that could aid your business. Likewise, if you do find an ideal spot, give them a call and return the favor.
- Comply with the ordinances and regulations that the local and federal governments impose. Pay your taxes, keep your records straight and ensure that you properly and adequately compensate your employees. If you incur penalties, pay them promptly to foster goodwill with the local authorities and avoid costlier fines for every delay.

4.9 Conclusion

The food truck business is not an easy one to get into due to all the legalities and permits that need to be obtained for it to operate. However, this is part of business, and this is part of your civil obligation to your government, regardless of your locale. Thus, compliance with these regulations ensures that you can continue your food truck operations smoothly and prevent any interruptions that could lessen the number of sales you can generate from the truck. Additionally, these would enable you to build the rapport necessary to ensure that you are in the good graces of the community that you serve, which could net you several advantages for your business. It's always good to be on the right side of the law.

5 Setting Up Your Food Truck

In the previous chapters, we dealt with the necessary researches, paperwork, and legalities that allow you to become the owner of a fledgling food truck business. At this point, you may have secured your financing and have fully committed to the industry. What's next? It is time now for you to delve into the nitty-gritty of the actual food truck itself and the items needed for your business to work.

5.1 The Truck

The core of the food truck is, from its name, a truck. However, a food truck does not limit you solely to the use of your truck as there are other forms of food trucks available, from food carts to even buses. The only limitations that exist are the regulations that permit such businesses to operate, so do your research into the regulations that your city has with regards to mobile food businesses and the use of trucks. Factor in the limitations of the size of your truck as well as the amount of storage you are permitted for water storage (both potable and waste)

On average, a food truck may cost anywhere from $70000 to $80000; however, these costs may vary on your decision if you want to purchase a new or leased truck or rent a truck. If you include the cost of equipment that you will need to fit into the truck, then these costs will increase. But first, where would you need to look? The answer depends on your decision, to rent or to buy?

To Rent or to Customize?

Apart from the ballpark figure in the previous section, it is entirely possible to start the food truck business with lower costs. In Chapter 2, we discussed the sources of funding for your business, and at this point, you will have viable options for your food truck. However, if you do not have much capital at the moment, it is entirely possible for you to start your business with a rented food truck. Sites such as www.roaminghunger.com/marketplace/lease-a-food-truck/ link with aspiring food truck owners, such as yourself, to lease food trucks that are suitable for your business needs.

Is it a good idea to rent? That depends. There is no surefire answer for this as this relies on your financial prospects and capabilities. It is not unheard of food truck owners to rent/lease their trucks from food truck companies as this is the more cost-effective practice with regards to the purchase of the truck and the equipment it needs to operate. The main draw for the lease of a food truck is the ability to pay in increments until you can obtain a new food truck yourself. This option is best for newbie food truck owners or restaurant owners who want to make their initial foray into the food truck business. The disadvantage for the leased food truck is that once your lease ends, you may have to return the truck used unless you renew the lease. If you do have to return the truck, this can cause a delay in operations or the closure of your business. A good practice for this is to ensure that you choose a company that allows for the renewal of your lease agreement or a lease-to-own arrangement. If in doubt, have your lawyer read the fine print for your ease of interpretation.

If you feel that purchasing a food truck is more your preference, the ballpark figure for the total costs was mentioned in the previous section. With the addition of the kitchen equipment and the need to fit them into the truck, this will add to the food truck's overall cost, which makes this the more expensive option and not ideal for the newbie.

However, this can go two ways. You can get a brand new one or a used one. There is a difference, though, aside from the more apparent use of words.

With the purchase of a used food truck, you ultimately save on costs and are basically given a trial run of how you and your crew can work in the space of the truck. Because the equipment needed is already present, you save on the time needed to decide. All you will need to do is ensure that everything is in working order; with the permits and licenses ready, you can commence business operations.

However, because it is used, it can be costly to maintain, and you may experience a few disasters such as engine stalls or the need for new parts for the truck, which can really cut into your costs depending on the severity of the wear and tear of the truck. Used food trucks, like used cars, do not have a long life expectancy, so in essence, you operate on borrowed time since you never know if the food truck will break down for good. Customization would be difficult as most food truck outfitters would need to know what they can work with, not work with what is already there. Sites such as www.roaminghunger.com/marketplace/buy-a-food-truck/ allow you to purchase used food trucks. Local options may also be available, so be sure to do a thorough search.

If you have your heart set on a new food truck, and you have the financials to see you through this endeavor, that would be the ideal option for you. Let's start with the disadvantages first: This is definitely the most expensive option there is, and because you are starting from scratch, business may not take off immediately because it takes time to retrofit the truck as well as customize it. If you want to make changes, it may have to wait due to the costliness of the new food truck.

However, a new food truck nets you several advantages, which includes full rein over the truck's customization to suit your needs, and you are assured that, unlike a used food truck, there is no wear and tear in the food truck. Because everything is new, you can save on repair and maintenance costs, and unlike all the other options, there are warranties for the new vehicle. Lastly, the aesthetics of the truck are more appealing as everything is polished.

If you do intend to purchase a food truck, there are several characteristics that you need to consider before you commit to a certain model.

- The smallest food trucks have a 10-foot bed. The bed of the food truck often increases in increments of 2 feet, with a maximum of 16-foot beds. To know what the best size for your business is, it is important that you are able to visualize the interior of your truck with your equipment with the help of a food truck fabricator. As you lay out your kitchen, be sure to pay attention to height, as you will need to account for shelves and storage and the wheel wells of the truck. You do not want to work in a severely cramped space, and it is bad practice to purchase a food truck and fit your equipment into it.

- Most food trucks are designed as a step van, which, unlike conventional trucks, are set lower and therefore allow you to reach your customers easily, and receive deliveries and supplies conveniently. Prices for this specific type of van may vary if you choose to rent, buy a new or used food truck. The price ranges for these models do not include the cost to convert the truck into a food truck.

5.2 Viable Sources for Food Trucks

The most logical option for you as a food truck business owner would be to approach your local dealership or a used truck dealership. To know what the most viable models are, you will need to do some research. Here is a brief overview of some of the more popular models.

- o The Ford Stepvan is the most familiar food truck model on the market. If you are unsure what this looks like, you probably have seen the UPS vans. If you did, then you have seen the Ford Stepvan. 1971 Models are recommended for their spaciousness. If you purchase

74

this second-hand, the price range is from $12500 to $31000.

- ○ Citroen H Vans are another popular model produced in France and are popular food truck models in countries like the United Kingdom. A second-hand Citroen H Van may range from $4000 to $25000.
- ○ Horse Boxes or Horse Trailers are ideal for small catering businesses and are popular for small events. The price for this kind of food truck can range from $1200 to $15000.
- ○ School Buses have a very distinct look to them and are also used as part of the food truck business. Because it is a bus, you have more room to maneuver in the truck for the prepping, cooking, and assembling of food in the truck. School buses may cost approximately $10000 to $50000 without conversion fees.
- ○ Airstreams resemble the familiar American Trailer and cost anywhere from $15000 to $93000.
- ○ Caravans are more vintage items that are easy to tow and store and are relatively cheap compared to the other options; these range from around $1200 to $9000.

There are other unique options for food trucks out there, which can be converted into mobile kitchens. Container Vans, Catering Trailers, and even Planes if you want something truly out of the box. While most of these are used, you can find a deal on new ones (except perhaps, the plane) through the use of sites like eBay or your preferred sites if you search online.

What will the Food Truck Run On?

It can be easy to say that food trucks run on gasoline, however, do not forget that at the back of the food truck is a mobile kitchen that certainly does not run on the same fuel as the food truck. To determine the main source of fuel for your food truck, you will need to account for the engine that your truck has, along with its expected mileage and the ease with which you can maintain it with the help of an available mechanic or service center. So, diesel engines or gasoline engines?

- A diesel engine has a reputation of being more long-lived and require lesser maintenance. However, it has a more complex mechanism than a gasoline engine, and despite your upkeep, it is quite costly to repair if it breaks down. Diesel engines provide more power, so this engine is suited for heavy-duty vehicles such as trucks and buses, which can save you on fuel costs due to its increased fuel efficiency. This is not ideal for a locale that has a cold environment as the diesel engines can develop a substance that would affect how it functions in the winter. Despite the reputation in how diesel engine affects the environment, an advantage with it is that it can make use of a biological alternative called biodiesel, which in turn is made up of used cooking oil.

- On the other hand, gasoline engines provide more acceleration for the vehicles but offer lesser advantages when compared to a diesel engine.

- Other options that are more environmentally friendly include the conversion of the truck's fuel source from gasoline and diesel to the use of natural gas. Although this is a more ecological-friendly and socially responsible move for your part as a business owner, the conversion of the food truck to this type of fuel source will need you to have a mechanic on call to troubleshoot any concerns with the operation of the food truck and its fuel.

- Hybrid options are also popular among step vans. There are manufacturers such as the Freightliner, which build trucks that utilize hybrid engines. Because of this, trucks equipped with hybrid engines are purported to reduce fuel costs by approximately 40 percent, and there is an expected reduction in the maintenance costs for the engine, estimated at a 30 percent decrease. However, if your food truck does not travel far, this engine is not recommended, despite its fuel efficiency. If you do not utilize a lot of fuel for your truck, this is not an economical option.

- The dawn of the electric vehicle has risen, and manufacturers such as Isuzu and Freightliner have created food trucks that run on electricity. Because of their relative novelty in the market, these trucks are quite expensive, with a cost of approximately $150 000. As with the hybrid engine, the electric truck's engine does not make for efficient usage of space, which can limit the amount of space you can use in your truck. Like the hybrid, electric trucks are not meant for businesses that travel great distances when their upper limit is estimated at 100 miles. Their speed is dependent on the amount of weight that the trucks carry.

This is just a section on what makes the food truck run and travel the routes that you have carefully planned. However, there is still the issue of the kitchen at the back of the truck and the miscellaneous equipment that are present. This more often requires the use of a different power source.

- Most kitchen equipments are designed to run on propane or natural gas. Propane, in particular, is favored due to its low cost, ready availability, and high energy output. Aside from this, propane tanks are the more environmentally friendly option and reduce the weight and noise in your truck due to their lightness. Propane gas has multiple functions as it can be used to heat up your grills and stoves and serve as a fuel source for your generators (you will really need one). It can also power the refrigeration units in the food truck. It does require careful maintenance and the need to check for leaks as propane is a highly combustible substance. Therefore, among the maintenance checks that need to be done would be to identify any potential gas leaks in the food truck just to avoid any mishaps.
- A Gasoline or Diesel Powered Generator may be the safer option if you are a little wary of the use of propane tanks, though this is less energy efficient compared to the propane tank. It is simpler, since the generator can utilize the fuel from

your truck as well. Be sure to keep a close eye on your fuel tank in this instance.

- o When you are in the market for a generator, there are a few factors to consider, which include the amount of wattage it can generate, the fuel source of the generator, price, service centers, and soundproofing.
- o **Wattage** can be computed through the formula volts x amps. You will find this in the manuals of your kitchen equipment. Add up the entire wattage of all the appliances that are expected to run on the generator with the addition of at least 15-20 percent of the wattage to be assured of a sufficient power supply.
- o Gasoline and Diesel remain popular options for fuel sources, though there are propane-based generators as well. Each model, ideally, must be able to run from the truck's fuel source.
  - Diesel generators are more commercially friendly due to their low maintenance and high fuel efficiency when compared to gasoline generators. These generators can also be made to run on biodiesel. A disadvantage would be the smoke that is generated by the diesel generator and the need for additional liquids in the winter to ensure it does not coagulate into a thicker substance.
  - On the other hand, the gasoline generator is cheaper and is lightweight compared to other generators in the market. However, it is not expected to be long-lasting.
  - Propane generators run on propane tanks, and if properly equipped, releases no carbon monoxide. However, it is not fuel-efficient as a generator.

- Solar Generators, while existent, simply do not generate the power in sufficient amounts to run the food truck.
  - Prices for generators depend on the wattage and the fuel source, and if you buy them new or used. While there are numerous brands to choose from, many food truck owners prefer the use of the Honda Generator. The price ranges from $500 to $10000 in accordance with how much electricity your food truck needs.
  - An important factor for the purchase of generators is the support it has in the event it encounters a problem. If you buy a generator, inquire about its support and if there are mechanics available to fix it.
  - Soundproofing is essential, especially if there are ordinances that prohibit loud noises. Hence, you will need to craft your own soundproof box for the generator with the use of either fiberboard or Homasote. Ensure that when you create the soundproof box, it is well-ventilated to prevent the build-up of fumes and overheating. Because of the fumes, you may need a pipe or an exhaust fan.
- Electricity is always a great option to power your food truck business, especially if you are able to book a catering event for your food truck for events where you can bring your food truck in. Most indoor venues do not permit the use of propane due to the high risk of carbon monoxide inhalation. Electricity will net you this advantage, as this broadens your business options rather than the limitations that you only can sell outdoors.

The Aesthetics

In the creation of your business plan, we have touched upon the subject of branding and identity of your food truck, as this is an essential part of standing out from the competition. By this time, you probably have the name of your food truck and what you want it to look like. The latter part is crucial as you want your food truck to be distinctive in the public's eyes. Think about Bob Blumer's Toaster Mobile, which incidentally is a mobile kitchen as well. For instance, if you sell toast, make your truck look like a toaster, with the corners of two slices of bread on top for an added panache. Here, you will want to work with a graphic designer to create the best aesthetic for your food truck. Why?

Décor Is Everything
The décor of your food truck is representative of the brand that it presents to prospective customers, and this is one of the means by which you attract customers to your truck. A distinctive truck can imprint itself in its customers' minds and cause them to instantly associate certain food with the visual impact of your truck, which can gain you more business.

The Essentials to Make a Food Truck Visually Impacting
Even though you may have some Photoshop or Photo Editing skills, a more professional look will scream to your customers that you are serious about your business, hence the need for a graphic designer who can create the aesthetics you visualize and apply them to your food truck. You have several options to choose from for the exterior of your truck, whether to have it painted or to have it wrapped. Wrapped? Yes, wrapped.

Painting
If you have a general idea of how to paint a car, then you are on the right track, as you can save on costs compared to hiring a professional and make this a team-building exercise if you want. A disadvantage to be had is that you are on your own if you design the food truck, and more often than not, it will eventually require a professional finish from a pro. If you are inexperienced, it would be good to have your food truck professionally painted. Most paint stores would have a general idea as to where your food truck can be painted, and look for the one that offers you a better deal and the equipment and facilities that can accommodate your food truck.

Vinyl Wraps
This is far more complex than what its name entails, as this is more than just wrapping vinyl around your truck. The wrap also functions as

a transit ad for the food truck, which is why its design needs to be on point with the type of cuisine that your food truck has on offer. Unlike painting, a vinyl wrap is quicker to apply on the food truck as it consists of a film that a truck wrapping company applies to the body of your truck. This is also considered the more economical means of decorating the food truck as this is more durable than painting. Most vinyl wrap companies have designers to help you come up with the design for your truck and warranties in case the vinyl gets damaged.

With the vinyl wrap, you have two options to choose from: Cast or Calendared Vinyl Wraps

- Cast Vinyl is a more durable form of vinyl that, with proper care, can last you several years. It also conforms to the dimensions of your truck to ensure that it fits perfectly. Most truck wrapping companies would recommend the use of this type of vinyl because of its material advantages. However, it is expensive but well worth the expense if it saves you from having to rewrap your truck at certain intervals.

- Calendared Vinyl is a less durable option as it only lasts for a few months at the most. Because it does not stretch as much compared to Cast Vinyl, this is only ideal for box trucks with a flat surface it can stick to, and therefore, your food truck's aesthetics may not be completely conveyed with this option. However, this is best suited for shorter displays and as a decal.

Windows

If you have seen food trucks, you will know that the window is another important aspect of the food truck's design, as this is the main point of interaction between you and your customers; therefore, you will need to make this section look nice. Counter space is always essential in your food truck, and this is highly dependent on your Point of Sale system. You can hardly expect an actual cash register on your food truck; therefore there is the need to streamline your window and window space.

The service window, as it should be called, can have two openings, where one window is for your customers to place their orders and pay, and the other window is to let the customers get their orders once their orders are ready. This is a dual purpose. It prevents crowds on both sides of the food truck and helps make the delivery of food and the taking of orders more efficient. It also prevents the cross-contamination of money and food. The service window is usually placed on the passenger side of the vehicle, although its placement can be up to your preference and its height depends on the height of the sidewalks.

Awnings

More often than not, the shutters that you open often double as your awnings for your food truck, and the most you can do is work with this. For those with service windows that are sliding, and do not use shutters, then the awning would provide a comfortable place for your customers to place and wait for their orders. The awnings, if used, should reflect the theme of your food truck to ensure cohesiveness in your concept.

Refrigeration

While this falls under the purview of kitchen equipment, your refrigeration equipment, especially your display chillers, can be used to entice customers to approach your food truck to purchase something ice-cold and refreshing. This would be your opportunity to upsell some of your food items to them. While not as visually impacting, it does appeal to the certain needs of customers to draw them towards your food truck.

Menus

In Chapter 2, we have discussed the importance of your concept and the type of food you wish to sell to the public. In this section, we talk about how to convert your concept into a menu that your customers will appreciate and one that will help ensure your food truck's success with the general public. Menu Crafting is deceptively simple because it is more than the assemblage of food items on a piece of paper. If you recall, there are certain analyses that are employed to determine the type of items that are popular and the items that are least popular, and because of this, your menu may undergo some changes in keeping with the concept of seasonality. Where do you start?

- Restraint is key. While it may be tempting to list down at least 10-20 dishes on offer, this is impractical in a food truck, especially since you have limited space to work with to make these dishes and limited storage for the ingredients necessary to the menu item. Therefore, you will need to streamline your menu and the items needed. A good idea would be to create a menu that uses similar ingredients so you can have a more efficient prep time. For instance, this can be the same garnishes, same sauces, and same wraps, with variations on the filling or protein. You will need to consider the equipment and power requirements needed to run them in the preparation of your dishes since you have limited space.

- Streamline your Menu. Your menu will need to focus on a limited or a more specific number of items. A popular practice among food trucks would be the use of threes – three main dishes, three sides, and three drinks that the customers have enough variety to choose from. When you do create a menu, ensure its cohesiveness with the theme. Nothing can be more irritating than approaching a Food Truck that promises, say, French Food, and it sells Tacos as a dish. It can be very misleading and would discourage your customers from returning.
  - Earlier in the book, we have touched on the Cost of Goods Sold. Use the concepts provided to ensure that your menu undergoes the changes needed to ensure your business remains profitable.
- Suppliers and Vendors are an essential part of your menu crafting for the reason that they are the source of your ingredients. The one disadvantage with the food truck is that the supply capacity is limited. You cannot order the ingredients in quantities equal to that of a restaurant, even with a commissary, unless you have a lot of storage. If possible, work with the ingredients that ensure continued profitability, and purchase items at wholesale or at food service supply stores.
  - For the supplies that you will need, it would be best to canvas your local vendors and see who provides the better deal. Some vendors may provide credit, which can be advantageous for you. Some vendors may offer lower

prices for premium ingredients which can be a steal. You just never know what you can find when you go explore.

- Sustainability is a key concept that applies to your food truck and the food and the community that it serves. If you can purchase your produce locally, this would be good for you and for your community. Check out what other farms and households have on offer; you may find produce better than what your wholesale store provides. This also has the added benefit of endearing you to locals as you support their business so that they can support yours too. A good place to start would be at www.ams.usda.gov/local-food-directories/farmersmarkets. Menu items that use these items would go over well with the locals.

- Consistent Recipes are key to an efficient menu. You may have them in your head, but you cannot be in the food truck all the time despite your best intentions. It is important to have these listed on paper with the right measurements to ensure consistent food quality throughout the food preparation. For this, work with weight (such as grams or milliliters) and use measurements (rather than season according to taste, or a pinch of – this can lead to inaccuracies as these are never consistent).

- Costs are always an important part of the menu crafting process, and with the unit on the COGS and the profitability of a menu item, consistently check your menu to see what can be changed and which menu items are more cost-effective. Research on what makes a reasonable price for food truck items, and when you cost, ensure that you are able to make change for your customers.

Ringing Up Sales

With the use of modern technology, more modern POS systems are available to streamline the order-taking process and the ease at which you can track sales in your food truck. The use of the POS system and, potentially, cash registers is dependent upon the ordinances of your local municipality if the use of a receipt is necessary. You may find this out when you apply for a business license for your food truck.

With the sales that you make, you need to establish a system that manages your cash efficiently. Money boxes are old-fashioned, and unless you are a whiz at math, it may lead to an inaccurate tally of your daily sales.

- How Do You Intend to Ring In Sales?

  There are several options to choose from, among which is the use of a cash register, which, though bulky, ensures stability in the way you can manage the money earned from the business and can issue receipts in accordance with local revenue laws.

  A Point of Sale System enables the ease of tracking your sales, the amount of cash received, and the inventory of items. It can be advantageous because of its versatility in cash and with sales paid with cards. A POS enables you to identify the fast-selling items on your menu. A disadvantage with this system is the use of a computer or a tablet; if any of these components fail, you stand to lose the data from the POS unless you have it backed up in cloud storage. This is not ideal, especially when it comes to taxes, when your records have to be audited. There are several POS providers such as HP and Dell, but as with other equipment, be sure to select a POS Provider that is not only easy to use but has the technical support you need in the event the POS System begins to glitch.

  Credit Cards and Debit Cards require the use of a Card Reader, as mentioned earlier on, for the convenience of customers who want to purchase items but have no handy cash, or if you land a large order, your customer can easily pay for these large sums. However, there are other options if you do not have a card reader, which include the use of sites such as **Paypal** to accept payments over the phone, or **Squareup,** which can offer discounts once you swipe the card. For these card readers, an important factor is the availability of an internet connection to ensure the stability of the payment process.

5.3   At the Core of the Truck: Setting up the Kitchen

The kitchen is the heart of the food truck business, and it is important that your kitchen can promote the efficient preparation of food and movement of you and your food truck crew as you take, prepare, and distribute the orders that come in through your service window. Thus, knowing how to set up the food truck kitchen is central to the operation.

How to Design an Efficient Working Kitchen in the Food Truck
The food truck's typical kitchen layout depends on the type of vehicle you have – a bus or a Step Van – and its size and dimensions. The kitchen layout also depends on the equipment you need and the amount of storage you want to have in the food truck. When you purchase or rent a food truck, the kitchen equipment may come with a design installed that can limit your customizations. If it does not have one, you have a blank canvas with which to consider how to layout your kitchen best.

- **Know The Workspace Limits**
   The kitchen is built at the back of the food truck, which means you have a very limited space to work with. Food trucks have a limited width of approximately 86 inches, which is around 7 feet. The length of the kitchen may vary, but the minimum is 10-feet in length. In a 7x10 space, you will want to adjust the layout of your kitchen, add the customizations you want, and account for the wheel wells of the truck, which can lessen the actual space you have to work with. Consider the disposal units, sinks, and fryers, which can also take up space in the food truck. Computer-Aided Design Programs provide a preview of your kitchen layout if you know how to use these; otherwise, consider the help of a Kitchen Equipment Specialist to help you set up your kitchen to your specifications and to promote the efficiency of movement within it. Kitchen designs are often governed by local ordinances, and it may be a requirement before you are granted a permit to operate a food truck. The

kitchen layout can be pricey, so it is best to get it done properly in the first instance.

- **Design with Efficiency in Mind**

  Think about how many people are there who will be in the food truck and the layout of the kitchen to promote their convenience in the performance of their tasks. For businesses that have all of their goods prepared in a commissary off-site (such as cookies and cakes), this is no problem, as one person can easily move in the food truck and take and distribute orders. However, for savory food trucks, where food must be prepared fresh, the cook must have ready access to the proteins, other ingredients, and kitchen supplies. At the same time, the assistant can help assemble the components that are ready. There must also be room for the cashier to take in orders and payments and arrange the tickets for the cook's convenience.

- **Choose the Right Equipment**

  It is hard to resist the purchase of kitchen equipment once you get to a kitchenware supply store; however, you need to remember the limitations of a food truck kitchen, particularly the amount of power that is needed to run appliances such as the refrigerator. You will have to downsize your ideas for a more compact model that can fit into the kitchen layout of your food truck.

  Kitchen Appliances may have warranties; however, you will need to identify if these warranties can be voided if these are used on a vehicle. Check manufacturers, and inquire about the use of their appliances in a food truck to be assured of this fact. Kitchen appliances will depend on the generator that you need to purchase; likewise, the generator will depend on the amount of wattage that your appliances will consume. This was discussed earlier on how to account for this. Once these are installed, ensure that they remain fastened to the floor of the food truck to prevent any accidents, and they are installed in a way that promotes easy clean-up and proper ventilation (especially for the equipment that uses gas).

- **Water Sources and Power Sources are Essential**

  We have touched down on the purchase of generators earlier, which are the main power source of your kitchen. Again, these generators would have to be soundproofed and well-ventilated to control the amount of noise and fumes generated as it functions. Generators that power themselves from the fuel tank of your truck are ideal.

  Other alternatives to power involve using a shoreline, which originates from a vending location that provides the electricity needed to run the food truck. This will save you on the fuel costs needed to run a generator while your food truck operates. Add outlets if you want to add additional smaller pieces of kitchen equipment as needed.

  Water sources are important as well as the means by which they are disposed of, which often takes place at your commissary. You will have to conform to the regulations specified in local ordinances as to the size and amount of water your food truck can carry. The type of sink depends on your needs, as it can have one or two compartments. Water sources may require the use of a water heater and a pump for the use of running water, so include these as you layout your kitchen.

- **HVAC**

  This stands for heating, venting, and air conditioning, which are necessary depending on your location. Venting is a must, as in the course of food preparation, it can get heated in the food truck; hence the use of an exhaust fan to vent would be a good place to start.

  Air conditioning units can cost additional power to run on a generator but are best used in warmer climates. However, these are not cost nor fuel-effective as they were not meant to be used in a food truck. The use of fans can double as the venting and cooling measures of the food truck, as these can draw away heat and fumes, especially if you are frequently cooking.

Set Up an Ideal Workflow Process

We touched upon the importance of a kitchen that promotes efficient movement. At this point, it would be necessary to identify specific work areas where each crew member would be assigned to. This can be done while the truck has not been retrofitted with your kitchen equipment. However, it would be ideal to do the workflow process to accurately simulate the conditions in the food truck so you can make the adjustments necessary.

- **Conduct a Test Run**
  It was stated earlier that in the food truck business, you have to open earlier than planned to iron out the wrinkles in the way your food truck operates. First, simulate how your food truck operates when it takes various orders in different combinations and how you intend to let your truck restock on the low food and supplies. Lastly, simulate (especially for health inspectors) how your food truck disposes of its waste.

5.4 Conclusion

The truck is the workhorse of the business, and the kitchen is the heart of the food truck. For smooth operations of the food truck, ensure that both can operate smoothly, and you would be able to generate the income needed to sustain your business and your employees.

6 Concepts: What Makes Your Food Truck Stand Out?

In the development of the business plan, it was stressed that you need to know what kind of food truck you intend to do before you come up with it. More importantly, what makes your food truck different from all the other food trucks out there in the street? The story behind a food truck can be a reason

6.1 Authenticity and Identity Matter, Show Off Who You Are

If you've watched episodes of the Great Food Truck Race, or if you have asked the owner of the food trucks what made them come up with their concept, you may receive answers that relate to their culture, their dream, something that was seen in their travels, or something that they felt was missing in the market.

Now would be a good time to know what you really want to do. If you are the only food truck in the area, great! If not, what makes you stand out? Do you have a secret family recipe for pasta sauce, barbecue, or burgers? Do you want to represent a lesser-known part of a culture with the use of regional cuisines? How would you know if there is a market for your products? It is not enough that you know how to cook; you need to know how to show it off with your concept.

- Research Pays Off
  As part of the creation of your business plan, you would have to convince prospective investors that there is a market for your food truck idea. At this point, you may have canvassed other food trucks In the area and conducted a feasibility study on the viability of your business in the food truck industry, and identified a need that you can fulfill.

- Identify the Right Niche for your Food Truck, as this will help identify the best hours for you to sell your food items. Do you intend to only cater to the lunch rush and breakfast crowd? Specific groups such as college students and faculty? Does your food truck sell in a part of town that has a predominant cultural minority? This will help tailor your concept into an idea that will appeal to these people.

- What Specific Part of Your Identity Will be on the Food Truck? If you happen to be a chef with a diverse background and want people to love your food, you need to let them know why you chose to do this type of cuisine. While the story does not need to be a tearjerker or completely inspirational, this helps your customers feel that they contribute to a part of your story when they eat your food.

- **Know Your Clientele**

One of the earliest tasks to be done when you make your business plan is the need to know your service's demographic and ensure that your concept is aligned or appeals to the target demographic. The local regional cuisine of other countries may appeal more to the palates of customers who are from that region, whereas more gourmet options may appeal to those who can afford to pay higher prices for a meal.
  - Office Workers and other professionals most often go for food options that taste good and are easily prepared due to the time constraints posed by their lunch break. Should these be your target population, your concept can target the morning commute, the lunch break, and snack breaks. Do not rely much on dinner time; if you have been in their footsteps, they are more likely to return home.
  - Tourists are more likely for concepts that present freshly prepared, clean food that is readily available. Remember that they are unfamiliar with the place and are more

likely to be found in tourist spots. Concepts that are popular are usually crowd-pleasers, and perhaps, more exotic offerings.

o The Late Night Scene offers a variety of customers, especially if your community has a bustling nightlife; customers are more likely to go for rich and gourmet food concepts that really go well with a nice cold drink.

o Do not discount parents with children. Remember that some restaurants have options for children with kid-size menus, so if you are in a place that has high foot traffic of children, it may be a good idea to offer their usual foods such as Tater Tots or Chicken Nuggets in smaller portions. In line with the initiative for healthy eating, ensure that there are healthier options available. It is important that your concept is able to win children over, as children are able to convince their parents to try food options that they normally would not try.

- **Meet The Demands of the People**
This does not refer to the customization of orders, though this is a valid idea. When you did your research, you have identified a need that has yet to be fulfilled in your community, and your food truck can fill that specific niche. However, one thing that customers would like to see from food trucks is transparency. If you have been to Japanese restaurants where the chef prepares the sushi in front of you, or a benihana restaurant where there is all the theater that comes with the preparation of the dish, this is the idea. Tableside service fits the bill as well. While this cannot be done in the food truck due to the lack of space, there is a certain amount of theater that needs to be involved in your food truck concept.

If you sell tacos, you can make a show of drizzling the crema over the finished product before handing out the order, or if you sell donuts, make a show out of the sprinkling of the other toppings like powdered sugar. This provides a bit of excitement for the customers, and subsequently, they feel that they can get their money's worth from your food truck concept.

6.2 Menu Craft

This does not deal with the prices, as this has been thoroughly covered in the computation and estimation of costs in previous chapters. Menu craft determines the items that go on your menu that can appeal to the public. In Chapter 2, an overview of the usual cuisines that are on offer and are generally popular to the public was provided. However, popularity is not a constant, and this is where your research comes in to create a menu that sells items that appeal to the public.

Make the Menu a Reflection of Your Idea

Menus are what customers look at when they want to see what your entire concept is about, and therefore, your menu should highlight the dishes that best showcase your concept. Generally, popular ideas that please American crowds include Burgers, Sandwiches (Nice Gourmet, Toasted ones), Barbecues, Hotdogs, and Tacos. For Canadian customers, this might depend on what is popular in the area, such as Lobster-based dishes, Poutine, or Regional Asian Cuisine. Similarly, British customers may find the appeal in a food truck that sells pies, pasties, and the ever-popular Fish and Chips, though a few Indian-themed menu items would not go amiss either. Indian customers may go for regional specialties, as well as vegetarian options that are available.

One flaw in most menus is that menus tend to be overcrowded with everything that is on offer. This is a terrible idea and a logistical nightmare as you and your crew will not be able to clearly execute the orders, especially if confusion arises from the menu items that are to be prepared. Because of this, streamline your menu to a few select items that best represent your idea.

- **Select Menu Items that Represent Your Idea**
  If you want to showcase the best of your cuisine, it is best to keep it at three main dishes, three sides and a drink or two to avoid confusion and ensure consistency in how the idea is

presented. Remember that you assemble and cook food in a limited space, so you would have to restrain your desire to ensure that you can consistently present menu items that are of the same quality as the idea you intend to deliver to the customer.

Refinement Makes All the Difference

When you look at a menu item, you can categorize your food items into several terms in accordance with their profitability after you compute the profitability of each item. A formula to help identify net contributions involves subtracting the Cost of Goods Sold from the Sales Price. A Weighted Net Contribution is computed through the formula No. of Items Sold x (Sales Price – COGS). With this, you would gain a more accurate idea of your best menu items and the items that should be swapped out. With these computations, you can categorize your main items into the following:

- **Prime Sellers** are your menu items that have a low COGS computation and are the most frequently ordered items by your consumer. Due to their popularity with your clientele, you will want prospective customers to purchase these items. For these, ensure that your food truck produces a consistent turn out of these items and that these remain the center of focus on your menu.

- **Standard Items** are just as popular as the prime sellers. However, they are in a different category due to the cost involved in making these items. A remedy is to either lessen the portion size or to increase the price to make up for the cost in making these.

- Items on the menu that do not cost much to make but are not as saleable as the first two categories are deemed **Sleeper Items**. Draw attention to these when possible, lower prices, or rebrand them to increase sales for these.

- **Problem items** are items that have relatively low sales and are expensive to make. If substitutions are made to the dish, it is possible to salvage the item. If this does not work, use this opportunity to put in a new dish.

6.3 Prices

The prices of the items on your menu are dependent on the computation obtained from the COGS. Earlier, two formulae were given to help you weed out which items are unpopular and identify your best sellers. Prices need to be adjusted, especially when you involve the seasonality of ingredients. This is where you can get creative with your dishes to substitute one ingredient that is expensive for a cheaper ingredient in season.

- **Calibrate Your Menu Prices to Your Clientele**

  One of the main tasks you have achieved is knowing who your customers are through your research. From that, you can derive the prices for your menu that you feel will be a reasonable price for your customers to pay. Office workers and professionals would be able to afford meals priced higher, but students and minimum wage earners may only afford the cheaper items due to budget constraints. Take the pulse of the public, and adjust your prices accordingly. Your customers will appreciate you for it and continue to patronize your business.

Profitability of the Menu Item

This is best done with the use of the Cost/Menu Analysis, where you need to use these formulae:

Food Cost = COGS / Sales Price

COGS = Food (the ingredients) + Paper (what the food item is served on)

Next, compute for the contribution margin of the food item to the food truck's profitability with the earlier formulae,

Net Contribution = Sales Price – COGS

Weighted Net Contribution = No. of Items Sold x (Sales Price – COGS)

These can help you refine your menu even further and let you know which items may need a price adjustment to help boost their sales.

Branding

The moment you had a business plan, you probably also came up with a logo and a catchy name for your food truck business. Aside from the brand name and logo, a few adjustments need to be made because this helps you put your food truck out there.

Your truck is the best form of advertisement out there, as the exterior carries your truck's name and shows what your truck is all about. Increase your visibility with a well-designed exterior and the use of strong, distinct colors. Be unique; there's an entire palette of colors out there for you to choose your design from. Also, since you cannot wash your truck all the time, make sure that your color is still visible under all the dust and smoke.

6.4   Visibility: Visual and Digital Impressions

The design of the food truck is another consideration, as an eye-catching design can attract customers immediately to your food truck (aside from the aroma of the food). Your vinyl wrap can not only carry your brand, but all the social media handles for your food truck that potential customers can follow. It would not hurt to add a QR Code on the truck's most visible parts. While the world is In the middle of a pandemic, a QR Code that generates a menu once scanned would help your brand and also your customers in the promotion of social distancing. There are QR Code generators available on the internet. Work with a graphic designer to ensure that it is made part of the Vinyl Wrap on the Food Truck.

If you plan on selling at night, the strategic use of exterior lights may help boost the visibility of your food truck. However, consult with local ordinances to ensure that you have the necessary permission to add the lighting to your food truck.

The Whole Package

Your brand can also be present in the way you present your food. Containers with your logo printed on them are excellent forms of brand promotion. Although, you will want to ensure that your food containers are of excellent quality. Make sure any coffee cups do not spill, cardboard containers are sturdy, and that takeout bags do not leak. These can make a world of difference with your customers.

Part of the way you present your package includes the way your menu is presented to the public. Your menu is one of the means by which you can communicate your brand to the public. Earlier, we mentioned the use of a Menu converted into a QR code that customers can easily scan to learn more about your food items. However, in lieu of this, you can also stick with the more traditional options such as the use of a menu board attached to the truck or in the form of a signboard that you can place in a conspicuous area to attract and direct customers to your food truck. The descriptions of your menu should convey what your dish is in a font that is attractive and easily read by customers. To ensure completeness, use a combination of the QR Code, a Menu Board, and a Printed Menu to ensure that you can maximize the exposure of your brand.

On the Web

If your budget permits it, a website would be a great way to ensure that your brand continues to interact with customers. A good website would have a design that reinforces your brand and has a layout that engages with customers. Important information that should be included in the website includes your food truck's usual route and schedules, your menu and its prices, the social media handles of your food truck, newsletters, if any, and content. WordPress is a popular and inexpensive option to start up a website for your truck. The website design should also be optimized for viewing on phones and tablets.

6.5 Conclusion

At this point, you would have your food truck ready for you to set up. You will know that as you set up, there are certain limitations that you as a food truck owner would have to work with, such as the ordinances and laws that govern the sale of food, as well as the limited space that you have to work with when you set up your mobile kitchen. More importantly, as the food truck is set up, you would have to build the brand that your truck needs and make it stand out from the moment you come up with a brand name and design for the truck.

Concepts and Brands are central to the success of your food truck, and with the right foundation, you would be able to generate the buzz needed to make your food truck a success. Therefore, for the food truck to succeed, your concept and brand must be solidified to make a concrete concept that leaves a lasting impression in the minds of your customers. This is a journey of trial and error, despite what you would learn from this book. Computations and analysis are important enough to determine which menu items need to be changed to ensure that your brand remains consistent and profitable.

BOOK 3: Operating the Food Truck Business: The Right Ingredients to Grow Your Business

7 The Bare Bones of the Food Truck: Inventory and Staff

Book 1 and 2 should have gotten your food truck up and running. It's time to get into the operations aspect of the business. There are several considerations that need to be made with the operations, including the number of employees you will need and the use of a commissary, suppliers, and a commercial kitchen. Earlier in the preparatory phase of the food truck business, the necessary legalities mandated by labor laws have been discussed and the forms that need to be filled up by your employees. In this section, we will learn about the roles each employee should fill in your food truck.

- **How many people do you need to hire?**

  While it is tempting to just do it all yourself, if you do fall ill, this would also mean the stoppage of your sales and the loss of the momentum you built. It is also tempting to hire a crew that can run your food truck 24/7, but your food truck needs to rest too. It is important to your operations that you can hire the most reliable workers for your food truck in an industry that usually has a high turnover of workers. Consider the space of your food truck because, remember, the food truck is a limited space, and you cannot crowd in there as this can lessen the output efficiency of your food truck and inconvenience your customers in the process as well.

  o **Cooks for Prep Work and For the Truck**

    You may need one or two cooks or chefs to help with the food preparation, although this is dependent on the concept of your food truck. One chef in the food truck can take charge of the cooking and the preparation of the food in the food truck, while one chef in the commissary can aid in the prep work to ensure that there is a steady supply of ingredients to the food truck. If your food truck relies on the sale of items prepared off-site, you may choose to have one chef who can prep and cook the items needed.

- ○ **Cashier and Front of the House Personnel**
  These are actually two different roles as these employees are located in different parts of the food truck. The cashier is inside the food truck and provides the change needed while the front-of-the-house personnel has the responsibility to attract customers to the food truck, take their orders, and help expedite them to the chef on board to ensure that these orders are made.

7.1 Educate Your New Hires on Your Idea

When you begin training your employees on your food truck concept, you will need to educate them on your idea. The advice in this book will help you find the best people for your company, but you'll still have to persuade them that your concept is worthwhile for them to dedicate their time to your firm. An essential part of a company's success is fostering a positive workplace culture and making sure your workers believe they have a significant role in your company's success.

Be the Best Management They Need

If you have worked or know someone who has worked in the hospitality industry, you may hear about management issues that caused the employee to leave, and you may hear the same from your interviewees. This may cause them to be dispassionate towards most businesses. Thus, it would be best to hire and pay them at a competitive wage. A higher wage than what they are used to ensures that you can obtain more responsible employees that your business can rely on. Aside from the use of a competitive wage, there are incentives to be considered. The food truck employees have more responsibilities than those in a traditional restaurant, as they would have to troubleshoot any problems with the food truck itself. The use of bonuses as an incentive is always a good idea and helps you keep your employees. A better idea would be the distribution of bonuses simply for a job well done. It shows your employees that you appreciate their efforts in making the food truck thrive. Aside from this, other incentives do not have to involve money; treat them to a movie screening or a beach picnic. Employees will appreciate the gesture and be more motivated to keep up the good work.

Customer Service is the Most Essential Skill

The success of your food truck, aside from the production of consistent, tasty, and speedy food, would also depend upon the customer service provided to your customers. Unlike the brick-and-mortar restaurant, food trucks do not stay in a specific area, and you may end up in neighborhoods that are unfamiliar with your food concept. So, you will have to win them over with customer service skills to ensure that your food truck remains profitable.

Customer service, then, is more exacting than that of a restaurant, purely because of the speed at which customers can spread the word about your food truck's reputation through the use of social media platforms. A bad review from a customer can easily ruin the reputation of your food truck. In line with this, you need to ensure that your crew can maintain a standard with which they deal with customers. Nice and speedy service and a friendly tone go a long way to ensure the continued patronage of your customers and the profitability you gain from your patrons and new customers. The attitude of the employee is a crucial factor for this, and those who can show empathy for customers are the ones who are best for your business.

Schedule Rotations

To ensure that your staff does not get exhausted throughout the operations of the food truck, create rotations or shifts to ensure that your staff can receive breaks, prevent their burnout, and ensure that they can try their hands at other aspects of the food truck (except for the chef/cook unless all staff members know how to prepare the dishes). This enables you to learn the strengths of your employees and prevent their boredom from the performance of the same tasks repeatedly.

Develop Policies for your Staff

This is congruent with the development of a culture in the company. As a business owner, you need to establish rules and standards that you expect your employees to follow, and this is covered when you train your employees. It is important that you focus on why you want your employees to perform in a specific manner rather than how it should be performed. This entails that the employee can understand the policies you have made with the truck and its operations and deters them from the use of shortcuts which could compromise the integrity of your business and the quality of the items produced. You also do not want to give your employees free reign over your business. To put it bluntly, you are a business owner, and you run a business. It is important to the success of your business that you impress upon your employees that you are still their boss, no matter how nice you are.

Policies should cover both the preparation of food and the driving of the food truck. Apprise your employees on the ingredients that go into your menu items and advise them to keep an eye out for potential allergens that may affect a customer's health. Common allergens that should be watched out for are soy, wheat, gluten, milk, and nuts. As for the driving of the food truck, ensure that you and your employees are able to undergo the needed driving tests for the reassurance that your employees can drive the food truck properly without any incidents. This latter part is important as accidents can mean either damage to the food truck, which can stop the entire business, or costly fees if the food truck damages other vehicles.

- Retrain when needed, at a regular schedule. Training should cover everything in your policy manual as well as a few what-ifs to gauge how well your employees will perform in a particular situation.

7.2 Inventories and Commissaries

The operation of a food truck will require you to have a commissary as your base of operations. When you apply for a permit to operate your food truck, you will be asked for proof of commissary as part of your application process. Firstly, what is this for? A Commissary and Depot are terms that are interchangeably used. A depot is simply a place where you can park your food truck for the night. On the other hand, a commissary is a gussied up depot which also functions as a site where you can prepare and store food overnight. This is important to your business as you will eventually need a place where you can store your truck and other supplies that you have bought in bulk, such as other dried items (flour, rice, spices).

Commissaries are present in cities with large food truck businesses, such as Los Angeles and New York. Other places where the food truck concept is still new may not have the commissaries your food truck needs, but you can remedy this by asking other food truck vendors in your area. If all else fails, look for alternatives such as large cafeterias, schools (especially culinary schools), and churches. Restaurants can also do double duty as commissaries if they are only open during a specific shift.

If you have the financial capability, it would be best to build your own commissary; otherwise, you would have to rent commissary space or make do with the other options available. If you intend to build one, obtain assistance from construction companies who have built-in accordance with the codes of your town. If you do rent a commissary, ensure that the price you pay is worth the services and amenities the commissary provides (adequate parking space, attendants, consistent power, cleanliness, access to water and ice, wastewater disposal, trash disposal, and the ability for the truck to be cleaned).

The commissary, as earlier stated, will be your base of operations. The commissary and its contents should be organized to facilitate the ease at which you are able to obtain a fresh supply of prepared ingredients and other accompaniments and exchange any waste products from your truck in turn. Your inventory is the main focus in your commissary, as you will want to ensure that you have an adequate supply of your necessary items. Restock your supplies when your inventory reaches a specific limit. To avoid waste, you must order a quantity sufficient to satisfy your needs.

- **Will You Do it Yourself? Or Let an Agent Do the Work?**

You have two options with the purchase of your items for your inventory: do it yourself, or do it through a purchasing agent. Regardless of whatever option you choose, an essential stage in the process is developing a list of inventory goods. Shopping lists are very different than creating a to-do list. Creating an inventory list involves the anticipation of the quantities of food and the specifics to ensure you get the right products.

- All the ingredients for your menu items should be on the list, with their specific variants. If you want Cuban bread, list it as Cuban bread rather than just bread. If you want pork, specify the cut needed.
- Categorize items to know what types of ingredients to look for group paper products together, as well as proteins, seasonings, dairy products, and starches. If you purchase these from the same supplier, it will save you money and the time needed to go back and forth to different suppliers.
- The list may not be as comprehensive as you want it to be, but make it as detailed as possible. Know how much you need before you find your suppliers
- While you compile your supply list, look for items that can provide more convenience on your part. Ready-made tortillas, for instance, or taco shells, pizza crusts, and sauce mixes can come in handy and cut down on prep time and costs with their added convenience. This is an option, but it is also economical.

Research Reappearance for Better Deals

Once you have determined the supplies and the quantities you will need for your food truck to operate, you will want to start looking for suppliers. When you search for suppliers, you want to look for suppliers with whom you can build a long-lasting business relationship with. You need to be able to trust them when they deliver the supplies that you need without their quality compromised. It is entirely possible to purchase some items from the wholesaler, and fresh produce from markets, as this is a way to be engaged in your community, who are also your customers.

- Ideal suppliers will be able to supply you with high-quality ingredients at a reasonable price. It is okay to work with numerous food suppliers as this is customary. Not all suppliers will have the items you will need for your inventory, so having access to other suppliers will help fill in the missing items in your list. Search for wholesale suppliers in your country, as these can provide discounts due to the amount of food that is distributed. If you find that their minimum amount is higher than what your food truck needs, collaborate with other food trucks who need the same ingredients and place your orders together. Sites such as www.sysco.com/ and www.usfoods.com/ are suitable for a start.

- Food truck owners and restaurant owners will be able to help you find local suppliers for the items you will need. Speak with them, and identify the best supplier for you based on their recommendations.

- Websites such as www.fastcasual.com/companies/directory/ and www.foodsupplier.com/ offer an online directory of food suppliers that you can filter to see which suppliers are nearer your area. Among the benefits of these directories is a brief description of these suppliers.

- Restaurant trade shows are a good place to glean information about food and restaurant supplies. You would be able to initiate a conversation with representatives from stores that catch your eye.

7.3   Identify Your Supply Sources

From the list above, you have made headway into locating the best suppliers for the needs of your food truck. At this point, you want to narrow down the list of possibilities to identify the best source of supplies from suppliers who can supply the ingredients at a standard that you require, in the quantities you need, and at a price that you find reasonable. To know this, a look at the supplier's facility is warranted so you can see how the supplier handles and transports goods. A clean and organized facility is the hallmark of a good supplier. If you see a dirty facility, skip it and avoid trouble with the health authorities too.

Ask how long the supplier has been in the business, and take this time to negotiate payment terms and return policies for excess items. Because of the pandemic, a good idea would be to inquire about online shopping options, and if so, are there minimum orders for supplies? Delivery schedules are a must to learn, especially since your operations depend upon the supplies of your food truck. More importantly, how does the supplier deliver specific items? Do they store meat and poultry in coolers while these are delivered? As a business owner, inquire about the supplier's discounts (this can be for bulk purchases, early payment of dues, cash payments, and the like).

Filter your suppliers according to how they answered these questions to know which supplier is the best one to work with. Once you have identified your supply source, this would be the opportunity to enter into further negotiations with your supplier(s).

- Price negotiation is an expected practice, especially for supplies. This can be done simply by asking outright if the supplier can provide a better price. Learn how to haggle over a price; it is a custom to reject the supplier's first offer. Accepting the first offer lets the supplier know that you would just accept any extra charges at face value. Trade concessions with the supplier, tit for tat, while starting with a low offer. Look for other perks your supplier may offer, such as extended payments and deliveries when the supplier sees fit at the cost of lower delivery fees.

- Item quantities are important, as you want to ensure that you are not a pound short on any of your ingredients. A good practice would be to give your supplier a copy of your supplies list so they do not have to bother you all the time with the type and amount. They can help you determine the amount you will need per week to avoid an oversupply of a particular ingredient.

- Payment terms are customarily within 30 days after you have received the items delivered. However, this is negotiable, and inquire with your supplier as to more flexible terms before you agree to contract their services.

- Delivery schedules are a part of the negotiation, so identify a time that is best for you and your supplier. Ideal times would be early in the morning, or the weekends, to ensure that you and your food truck are not on the road.

Once you have established a relationship with your supplier, ensure that you return the favor through the prompt payment of your dues to them, invitations to visit your food truck if you're nearby, and keep them in the loop with any occurrences in your food truck.

Every Item Counts

To be safe, it is crucial to estimate the number of days the inventory will last. This will let you calculate how long your list will last. You need to remember two formulas: These transactions are a two-stage procedure, and you will require your financial statement for each phase:

- **Average Daily Food Cost = Food Cost / No. of Days in Period (the no. of days you sell)**
- **No. of Days in Inventory = Ending Food Inventory / Average Daily Food Cost**

Once you have managed to compute the Number of Days in Inventory, you should have approximately 3-5 days' worth of food in your inventory, which is to be expected in most food trucks. Any value above this will indicate that you have ordered excess inventory, and this could lead to wastage of resources that can hurt your business in the long run. Lowering the amount you have in excess will lead to lowered food costs.

The use of a spreadsheet to help tally your daily food costs would be useful to help you keep control of your inventory and lower your food costs when necessary.

Prevent Inventory Loss

This is to be an expected occurrence no matter how much you have vetted your employees. Here are a few examples:

- The under-ringing of sales through the alteration of prices by the employee, who inputs a lower price into the register, and keeps the remainder.

- Tampering of Order Tickets, where the employee disposes of the order ticket and keeps the money earned from that order.
- Theft of Food and Office Supplies, which can seem inconsequential but can set back your costs over time.

This is best prevented by encouraging customers to ask for their receipts after each order and ensuring that the cash register is locked after every transaction, with its key in your possession. Involve your employees in ways theft can be prevented. On your part, ensure that you perform a thorough background check on your employees and keep the amount of cash in the cash register low. This will make the potential thief think their time would be wasted stealing from the register. Lastly, conduct random checks to ensure that everything is in place and spot checks on your inventory.

Efficiently Manage Waste from the Food Truck

Keeping the precise amount of items you need to prepare your menu items is always a good idea as you ensure that you do not waste any of your ingredients or throw away any spoiled or ruined ingredients, which results in a loss of money and a loss of sales for the unsold items.

- To prevent this, it would be important to go back to the inventory and ensure that you can order the appropriate amount of ingredients, enough at least for a two-day supply to minimize food waste. Ensure that the items delivered are of the right number and of the right quality.
- If you receive wilted produce or dubious-looking meat, look for a different supplier.
- Remember FIFO (First In, First Out), use the older items in your inventory.
- Store items properly because substances emitted by fruits, for example, can cause other produce to mature faster, and therefore, spoil faster. Dry goods should be kept tightly sealed to prevent spoilage.

8   Preparatory Measures

You have your truck, staff, inventory, and ingredients, so the next step deals with food safety. Food safety is a critical concept in the hospitality industry as improperly handled and prepared food can jeopardize your employees' and customers' safety. It can potentially close down your business due to health code violations. This chapter shows you the important steps needed to ensure that your food remains safe for consumption.

8.1   Let Safety Be Your Guide

The last thing you want in your food truck is a customer who gets food poisoning after eating your food. Raw food can be contaminated by various bacteria and parasites (Salmonella in Raw Chicken, Trichinosis in Raw Pork for one), so knowledge in food safety can help protect you and your customers from illnesses sustained from these improperly prepared or stored foods. There are ordinances that your food truck and commissary are expected to comply with, and food safety seminars are mandatory for employees entering the food service industry. Learn more about these by asking your local health department for their guidelines.

- **Inspections**

  Health inspectors routinely check out food establishments to check for continued compliance with food safety regulations and will penalize you with fines for lapses in food safety. Keep an eye out for them and avoid any problems by keeping your perishables stored safely and ensuring a clean workplace in your food truck.

- **Training Pays Off**

  As mentioned earlier, employees in the food industry are mandated to attend seminars on food safety. Ensure that they have complied with this requirement and ask for a certificate that permits them to handle food. Aside from this, conduct your own training on food safety, especially with the safe handling of food.

- **Wash Frequently**
  The CDC and the WHO both have stated that the simplest method of preventing contamination and infection in any setting would be the use of hand hygiene. Simply, always wash your hands, especially before and after you handle raw and prepared foods. This is best done with the use of warm, running water and soap. Wash your hands up to your wrists for approximately 20 seconds (This is the same length as singing Happy Birthday twice). Dry your hands on a clean towel and prepare to do your next task.

- **Ensure that the Produce is Clean and Properly Stored**
  The primary cause of food-borne illnesses is food-borne bacteria which can be found in food that has been improperly cleaned and stored. Because of this, the storage of food at the appropriate temperature and in the right receptacles can help stave off the growth of these organisms. Among the most prevalent causes of food-borne illnesses are:
  - *Clostridium botulinum* is an organism that can cause a condition called botulism, a condition that causes the paralysis of the muscles and can often be fatal. This can be found in the soil, water, and in the intestinal tracts of seafood and animals. If you use canned goods, avoid those with dents or bulges as these are more likely to harbor the botulinum toxin in large quantities.
  - *Escherichia coli* is a common bacteria that can be found in unpasteurized milk, unpurified water, and, at times, in the intestines of animals as that is its natural habitat.
  - *Salmonella* is a classification of several bacteria that form the most common cause of food-borne illnesses,

especially from the consumption of improperly cooked eggs.

- o *Listeria* is another classification of organisms found in unpasteurized milk, leafy vegetables, processed foods, and intestinal tracts.
- o *Hepatitis C* is a virus transmitted via the fecal-oral route, and while not found on food, it can be found if you use unclean water to prepare your food items.

These are just some of the various microorganisms that can cause food poisoning in improperly prepared food. Produce should be thoroughly washed and inspected for any remnants of dirt, especially if you use cabbage and other leafy vegetables and root crops. Meat, poultry, and seafood should be inspected for freshness. Dairy products, in turn, should be properly stored, sealed, and pasteurized.

Aside from the fresh application, the same bacteria can grow on food that has been cooked and left to stand. Once the food is cooked, do not leave it to stand. Either serve it immediately or store it and serve whenever possible. Refrigeration can only retard the growth of microorganisms but not completely kill them. The microorganisms can only be killed with the use of proper cooking techniques.

- **Frequent Sanitation is the Best Practice**
Sanitation is the term used to refer to the process of cleaning equipment, which includes the need for your workspace to be clean. It is a bad idea to let your food defrost on the kitchen counter. If you must defrost it, place it in the refrigerator ahead of time so it can gradually thaw, or use a microwave. This also prevents the run-off of the meat and blood from the counter into the rest of the food truck. Sanitation will apply to your utensils, which must be washed with hot and soapy water. If possible, use bleach on them to sanitize, but this is optional. A clean workplace will ensure your compliance with health codes if a health inspector comes to visit.

- **Frequent Inspection is Always a Good Idea**

Aside from the inspections conducted by the local health inspector, it would be good practice to supervise your employees in the way that they handle and prepare food at regular intervals and at random to see if they adhere to proper food handling standards. Predict your Inspectors' moves by ensuring that your food truck and the employees maintain the proper cleanliness and food handling standards.

Health inspectors enforce the health codes of your local government. This enforcement includes the inspection of places that sell food and issue penalties according to the health code violations observed upon their inspection. Health inspectors often look for the following practices:

- The performance of hand hygiene as you handle and prepare food.
- The food that your food truck sells is sourced from a reputable food supplier with the right licenses.
- The food that you cook has been cooked at the right temperatures (which will be elaborated on later)
- The prevention of cross-contamination between raw food and cooked food items.
- Miscellaneous observations include the inspection of labels (discussed later on in this chapter), your permits to operate, thermometers that have been calibrated to read the right temperature, and the overall cleanliness of the surfaces of the food truck.

You and your employees may be quizzed by the health inspector on several topics related to food safety. These include:

- The proper storage of produce at the right temperatures,
- if you use any pre-made or pre-prepared food and how you reheat and cook them,
- temperature control and how you maintain these,
- how you handle potentially dangerous food items (seafood, eggs, etc.),
- if you make your food from scratch and how you label your inventory,

- policies on the handling of cooked food and on hand hygiene and gloves,
- the usage of pest control services,
- policies on employee illnesses and injuries, and
- lastly, the onboarding process for new hires and their food safety compliance.
- **Did Your Inventory/Commissary Research Pay Off? Approved Food Sources**

  Your Suppliers and Commissary Researches should yield you the best suppliers who can provide high-quality ingredients at reasonable prices, as well as a commercial kitchen space that is clean, has running water, and the needed items to help clean the kitchen area. If your supplier delivers substandard inventory items frequently, change suppliers. Likewise, check if your commissary is also up to health code standards with waste disposal and wastewater disposal for your kitchen space and food truck.

The Right Temperature for Everything

Food must be cooked at precise temperatures if you want the microorganisms in them to be killed. While there are raw applications of food such as sushi and sashimi and even ceviche, these are exceptions. The following table lists down the various temperature that food can be cooked.

Temperature in Degrees Fahrenheit	Meat
145	Steaks; Veal, Lamb and Beef Chops
160	Pork, Ground Veal and Ground Beef
165	Ground Poultry
180	Whole Poultry

To gauge this, the use of a kitchen thermometer would be helpful to learn if a piece of meat has been thoroughly cooked. Infrared thermometers can be used if you can get them; otherwise, insert the probe of a meat thermometer into the thickest part of the meat to learn if the meat has reached the recommended temperature.

Temperature control is an important process. Hot food should be kept at 140 degrees Fahrenheit or lower, whereas cold foods at a temperature of 40 degrees or lower. If items have been thawed, use them promptly to prevent the growth of bacteria. In order to store perishable goods optimally, your refrigerator should be set to 40 degrees F, and your freezer should be set to 0 degrees F. Avoid filling the fridge to the brim since this prevents cold air from circulating throughout the refrigerator promotes bacterial development.

If you must reheat prepared food, a temperature of approximately 165 degrees Fahrenheit is sufficient to kill any bacteria that has made its way onto the food.

Prevent Cross-Contamination

In cross-contamination, germs that have spread from one food or utensils are transferred to another food, utensils, or objects. Improperly handled foods may lead to cross-contamination in your food truck, and this might lead to your food truck being covered with germs.

With limited working space for food preparation in your food truck, one of the foremost concerns with food safety relates to the potential cross-contamination between raw food and prepared food. No matter how cautious you and your employees may be, there is always the risk. Although there are measures to prevent cross-contamination of food. The methods to minimize the danger inside the food truck are:

- Always perform hand hygiene within a 20-second duration every time you handle food in any state (raw or cooked).

- Wash all the unpacked produce under running water before you serve it, prep it, or cook with it. Firmer items such as potatoes and melons can withstand scrubbing with a produce brush. Dry with a paper towel to inhibit the growth of bacteria directly on the produce.

- In the preparation of food, always keep raw and cooked food on separate platters and on separate chopping boards. Similarly, replace your chopping boards if they start to develop indentations, grooves, and other deformities. These can be breeding sites for microorganisms that have not been completely washed away.

- Cooked food should never be placed on a surface that once held raw food, especially if it is raw meat, seafood, poultry, or eggs. Trichinosis, E. Coli, and Salmonella may spread onto the cooked food, which would make cooking it a waste.

- Seal raw meat items in a resealable container to ensure that their juices do not contaminate other food items. Store these on the bottommost layer of your freezer.

- For sauces and marinades, keep them in separate bowls if you intend to use them to baste the meat, seafood, or poultry as it cooks. Alternately, you could also boil the sauce or marinade.

Labels Do Efficient Work

This is a relatively simple concept. Once you receive your delivered items in inventory, a good practice would be to label each item according to the date that you received them. This ensures that you maintain an orderly inventory, with the older items in stock used first and the newer items saved for later. With the promotion of food safety, labeling also ensures that the items you use are fresh and well within their predicted expiry date. This reduces the potential food spoilage and wastage and saves you on food waste costs, as well as wasted inventory and sales losses.

Permits, Licenses, and all the Paperwork

Before you have even begun the entire food truck process, one of the earliest items you have to obtain is the necessary permits, which have been discussed earlier in this book. Create a checklist from those items to determine if you have covered all your bases before you begin your food truck operations. In case you are not present in your food truck, have copies of these made to ensure your employees can present the necessary papers upon request by any authority of where your food truck operates.

8.2   Do You Have the Right Equipment?

In the restaurant business, your equipment and other kitchen paraphernalia are referred to as the batterie de cuisine, defined formally as the range of tools used to prepare your food. By this time, you have obtained all of the larger equipment such as flat tops, broilers, grills, stoves, ovens, and deep fryers. However, there are smaller items as well needed to ensure the completeness of your food truck. Look at the table below to see if you have the needed items for your food truck and commissary.

For Prep Work	For Cooking	For Frying	Other Equipment
Can Openers	Broilers	Fry Baskets	Warming
Rolling Pins	Charbroilers	Deep Fryers	Ovens
Blenders	Ovens	Oil Filtration	Holding
Food Processor	Crepe and	and Disposal	Cabinets
Knife Sharpeners	Waffle Makers	Units	Ice Machines
Mandolins	Flat tops		Refrigerator
Meat Grinders	Cook Tops		Pots
Meat Saws	Grills		Pans
Mixers	Panini Presses		Spatulas
Weighing Scales	Microwave		Whisks
Thermometers	Ovens		Knives
Kitchen Timers	Pizza Ovens		Oven Mitts
	Rice Cookers		Ladles
	Pasta Cookers		Tongs
	Steamers		
	Toasters		
	Rotisseries		

These are just a small percentage of the equipment you may come to need in your food truck and your commissary. However, this is a section on food safety, so do ensure that when you purchase your equipment, they are also safe to use. Electrical appliances, in particular, should be properly insulated and can prevent grounding.

Another often overlooked aspect is the cleaning supplies that you will need for your food truck and commissary. These include the following:

Cleaning Supplies
All-Purpose Cleaner for the Walls and Floor of the Food Truck
Brooms
Degreaser
Glass Cleaners
Mops
Oven Cleaners
Soap
Sponges
Sanitizers
Stainless Steel Polish
Paper and Cloth Towels

However, some of the items may be a bit costly, but they are worth the price with the convenience they afford you and save you time (and back pain) from bending over and scrubbing flat tops, ovens, and the like from the messes that are made in the food truck. Care should be taken with the use of these chemicals, as some of them are too dangerous to be kept in the food truck. These should be stored, mainly in your commissary. Because these are chemicals, ensure that your employees know the proper first aid procedures in the event that these chemicals are ingested or come into contact with the skin.

Cleanliness

The experience of a food truck involves the sale of delicious food items to customers; however, the overall impressions that your customers gain from your food truck are just as important as the food. Because of this, if your food is good but your truck is messy, this can lead to a negative experience that makes the customer doubt that the food they bought is not contaminated with waste. This is why the cleanliness of the food truck is just as important as the food you put out (aside from the inspections from the health department).

In the previous section, the various paraphernalia to maintain the truck's cleanliness has been listed as a guide. Employees are expected to clean the truck during their shift and after the end of their shift. The last part ensures that the truck is ready for use the next day. What makes a clean food truck? It is more than just cleaning the floors and walls of the truck and washing the pots, pans, and utensils used. It is expected that while you clean your food truck, that the following tasks are also performed:

- Cleaning the grill in between cooking meats, poultry, and seafood.

- The cooking line should be given a thorough wipe down. This extends to the prep areas in the food truck, and by extension, the kitchen in the commissary.

- Change cutting boards. This helps prevent wear and tear on one and ensures that you work with a clean cutting board for prep work.

- Dispose of your trash in public dumpsters.

After these tasks have been performed, it is expected that at the end of the shift, cleaning is performed on several areas, which can include the fryers - including the proper disposal of used oil; the microwave - if you have one, clean the outside and inside; grills are to be brushed, wash, and sanitize all other utensils with the use of warm, soapy water. Empty any containers and clean their receptacles. Cover bins with plastic wrap. Wash the mats; lastly, sweep and mop the floor of the truck.

Daily cleaning tasks for the food truck involve the care of the grill and the change of foil linings on any heated implement you use in the food truck. Wash can openers if you use them, and clean the hood filters.

Weekly cleaning tasks include removing empty coolers, cleaning sinks and faucets of the mineral deposits around them, cleaning the other machineries in the food truck, and maintaining the sharpness of the knives and seasoning of the cast iron pans if you use them.

Recommended monthly cleaning tasks include cleaning the backs of the ovens, stoves, and fryers to prevent the buildup of grease, which is a fire hazard. Clean out your freezers, and empty and clean any ice machines. Check your ovens and thermometers if they are still able to detect the right temperatures. Walls and ceilings should be washed by this time. Any storage areas should be cleaned out. To promote the continued safety of your employees, restock your first aid materials (it would be best to have an inventory of this as well), and update any information regarding the use of chemicals in the food truck. If possible, have a list of antidotes for chemical ingestion on hand. Yearly, the exhaust hoods should be cleaned (preferably by professionals), update your fire extinguishers and fire suppression systems in your truck, clean the pilot lights, have your truck inspected by exterminators to eliminate any pests.

How Well Do You Know Your Business?

This is often the part where your knowledge about your own business is evaluated, and something you should ask yourself every time your food truck sells your items. Before you commence your operations, you will want to do a run down to ensure that the operations of your food truck go as smoothly as possible.

- **Before Everything Else**

  Key Performance Indicators are a necessary tool to help you identify the benchmarks that your food truck should aim to achieve or surpass. With this, you will be able to determine if your business is breaking even or if you are operating at a loss. Among the most important indicators of the success of your food truck once it begins operations are the sales performance and the kitchen performance. Earlier on, various formulae were given to help you identify profitability, and this is where these come into play. Focus on your Percentage of Food Costs, the number of sales made per week, the cost of your inventory, a menu analysis of your most and least profitable items, and the number of sales per head.

  The number of sales per head is computed as: Total No. of Sales/No. of Customers Served.

  Compute your staff's costs for your staff, which include your total labor costs, hours of labor, and turnover rate.

To evaluate how effectively your food truck works as a company, get input from your customers and staff. This can let you have a good idea of the likelihood of your business's success and where it may still improve.

8.3   Is Your Food Truck Maintained?

Before you set off in your food truck to begin your dream of selling food, you need to ensure that all safety aspects have been addressed, including your truck. Not the kitchen, because this has been covered earlier on in this chapter, just the truck itself. If you have owned a car, you will know the necessity for frequent tune-ups and maintenance, more so if you chose to rent or buy a used food truck. There are several items that you and your employees should be able to check in your food truck to ensure that it is in its best shape:

- Oil Changes, particularly if your food truck reaches a certain mileage.
- Fluid Levels, which are best checked manually, rather than relying on the indicators on the dashboard.
- Tires, which require inflation to a proper pressure per square inch ratio, to ensure safety and savings on fuel costs.
- Checkups for your food truck's equipment must be done by a licensed mechanic and certified by the Department of Motor Vehicles (DMV).
- Extra Supplies, such as a tool kit, jumper cables, extra oil, just so you and your crew would be able to deal with any mishaps that can occur while on the road.
- Insurance, to keep all your bases and risks covered while your food truck is on the road.

Have a reliable and trusted mechanic perform regular check-ups on your truck and replace parts whenever you are advised to. This will depend on your mechanic's assessment; it will save you on costs in the long run and prevent the loss of income should the food truck begin to malfunction. Ensure that the mechanic you have chosen comes recommended by other food truck owners and has the certifications needed to work on your food truck's specific make and model.

Aside from this, ensure that your employees know what to do in the event of a vehicular emergency. They should know to pull to the side of the road and know how to change tires if need be or signal for help if there are other problems. It is important that your employees know how to keep your food truck and themselves safe from any damage or injuries while on the road.

Do You Have Your Papers in Order?

Lastly, before you begin operating the food truck, check if you have all the necessary permits, and as advised earlier, make sure you have copies of these permits in your office and on the food truck. These ensure that in the event of an inspection by any authority, that you do have the permits to operate, sell food, park, and conduct business in the area. This would save you time dealing with these issues and money from any penalties. Once you have made sure of these, it's time for the food truck to hit the streets.

9   Make the Most of Marketing: Best Strategies for the Food Truck Business

Your food idea may be the most novel one out there, and your food can be unique and delicious in its own right. However, without the right marketing strategy, all of your efforts would come to naught. Why? Earlier on in this book, you may have done your research on the customers who would buy from your food truck. You cannot rely on foot traffic alone to fuel your business. You need to develop strategies to attract more customers to ensure your business gets the required recognition.

•   Research, Research, Research

When you created your business plan, we emphasized that you need to do some research to figure out your target demographics population, your ideal areas of set-up, your competition in the food truck business, and several other analyses. All of these are necessary prerequisites and aids you in doing proper research. Knowing your target population ensures that you can develop a marketing strategy that appeals directly to the target population. However, there are several other factors your research needs to address.

- **Know Your Competition's Strengths and Weaknesses**

  For instance, your competitor is a savory food truck that brings in many customers – this would be its strength; however, this food truck does not do desserts. That is a weakness for them. If you can dive into using a dessert truck, this would be a prime opportunity to take advantage of their strengths and weaknesses and make it work for you. Since they attract customers in this example, try to speak with the food truck owner and ask if they would like to collaborate, they sell savory items, and you can provide the desserts, which makes use of their weak points.

- **Know Your Opportunities and Threats**

  Using the same example in the previous bullet, you can take advantage of this opportunity to promote your dessert truck and generate more sales for your business. This is another way to establish linkages with other food truck owners. Not everything has to be a cutthroat competition; collaborations with other food trucks are opportunities that you can look out for. Threats will arise from your assessments, such as a similarly themed food truck or ordinances that restrict the operations of your food truck to a certain time.

Knowing these would enable you to come up with a definitive marketing strategy that would help generate the business that your food truck needs to gain profit. So, let's talk about how to create a reliable marketing plan that puts you on the roadmap to succeed in your business;

9.1   Marketing Plans

You cannot just barge into the food truck business without any form of marketing strategy. Therefore, come up with a marketing plan that will not only attract and engage with your target audience but will delight your prospective customers to trust your business to provide a certain quality either in terms of taste or customer service. Not having a marketing plan from the start might prove fatal to your business as you won't attract enough customers. When you develop a marketing strategy, this would need to be consistent with your brand, your concept, and needs to appeal to the target population. Your marketing plans should be able to hone in on the message or problem your food truck intends to address. Create a marketing plan that answers your customer's needs, not your food truck, because this plan is all about your customer. First of all, to make any strategy for your food truck, it is crucial to have a single clear message about what type of food you will provide and the kind of cuisine that your consumers are after. Once you have a solid marketing plan and a description of your business, it's time to broadcast it to your community.

- **Public Relations and Media Matters**
  To ensure that your message gets done professionally, the use of a Public Relations Firm would be a great help. You need to approach the right channel to help you create a cutting-edge plan. The success of your approach will depend on your edge against other food trucks. However, this cannot be accurately measured because it is difficult to determine if the person went to your food truck because of the PR Campaign, the Ad, or simply chanced upon it.
  Public Relations Firms have the benefit of generating the hype about your business even before you open. These create a reputation and image that the public will associate with your

food truck. As a result, Public Relations Firms help boost not only the hype of your food truck but also its reputation once it has become established as part of the industry. Their purview lies mainly in the form of press releases and website updates. Press releases, in particular, are prone to misinterpretation, so your PR firm must use an experienced and credible journalist should the need arise.

- o PR Firms often handle press Releases, but if you want to do this yourself, your Press Releases must include the following elements:
  - A Headline or Title that would grab the attention of the reader.
  - The Date and Place
  - An Introduction which answers the Who, What, When, Where, Why, and sometimes How?
  - The Body should elaborate on the topic discussed during the introduction, which is best illustrated with a few quotes from you as a business owner.
  - A Boilerplate – a term used to refer to a brief background about you and your company: this should be kept short, with a maximum of two paragraphs.
  - Contact Information which will include your name, business address, and any social media handles as well as email.
  - Endings are marked with three hashtags to indicate that this is the end of the press release.

Advertisements can take on several forms, whether if it is in print, radio, or media. The main disadvantage with ads is that they are always paid compared to PR and Social Media. Therefore, the business can generate less through ad placement. There are still other ways to generate buzz through this. You will get a glimpse of it in the next section.

If you choose to do it yourself, read about what captivates your consumers, and use this information to create a message that you can share with your customers. Once you have crafted a unique message (such as, if you are the only food truck that does a particular cuisine or the first food truck in your area), share it wherever possible to generate your hype. Do not be afraid to ask for help from friends in the industry, food truck, or media. This is the time to put your business forward and make sure your business gets launched in the best possible way.

- **Host Events**

  To gain customers and generate business, you need to engage with your community. There are numerous opportunities to achieve this, such as using the strategy in the previous section. Before your food truck opens, visit media outlets throughout your area. Invite over TV, Radio, and Print Journalists, as well as Food Bloggers for a free tasting of the items in your food truck. The cost of feeding them can offset the amount you have to pay for advertising, and this puts you in the good graces of the media who can generate the buzz your business needs at the cost of free food in the tasting event.

  You can also join in with other food truck owners and create your event, which will attract customers. If you're a Mexican Food Truck owner, host a Cinco de Mayo event. Opportunities abound to host events that engage the community, and hosting events can help you capitalize on potential customers.

- **Link up with Apps**

  This is often associated with the use of Social Media Apps. Still, other apps that involve food delivery are also a viable means to increase the exposure and accessibility of your food truck, important while the pandemic is still ongoing. If your customers are unable to get your food, the food delivery apps can take your food to your customers. See if these apps can promote businesses as well, or if they have a recommended list and inquire how to get on the list.

- **Have a Website**

Creating a website is generally inexpensive, provided you have the right content to back it up and the use of Search Engine Optimization and unique keywords that would yield your food truck if a customer searches the Internet. PR firms can manage websites to post press releases. If you are on your own, sites like WordPress can create websites for free. Don't forget to drop the link into your social media accounts to promote customer engagement.

- **Social Media is Always a Good Idea**

  Compared to traditional media platforms, the use of social media is relatively new. However, with a large percentage of the population having access to the internet, it makes sense to engage them on a favorite platform. Create a social media page for your business, and use **Facebook** to boost your business for a specified time, at a cost within your budget. Similarly, **Twitter** can let your regulars and other customers know where your food truck is at a specific time of the day. **Instagram** can be used to promote food posts and draw customers to your food truck. **Foursquare** can be used to boost your business and showcase your menu items to your customers.

  Twitter, in particular, has a limited number of characters that can be tweeted, 160 to be precise. So, if you choose to use this, keep your message distinct and use #hashtags when possible. Augment your posts with pictures to engage with other Twitter users.

  Social media can also be used to promote online reviews on your chosen platforms. Customers can leave reviews on the social media pages of your business, and you can use these reviews to obtain ratings and recommendations according to the social media platform used.

- **eMail Newsletters for Frequent Fans**

  This is best utilized if you have a website or blog that customers can visit. The number of times that customers visit your site can lead to further engagement. Give an option where they can subscribe to updates from your food truck directly into their email notifications to promote your business. Use this opportunity to know who your regular customers are as well.

- **Host Contests**

    This is a marketing gimmick that often generates excellent results. Contests on special occasions like the anniversary of your operations or if your truck is about to hit a particular milestone can generate anticipation for your business for customers who want to win that extra incentive that is on offer. The prize does not have to be expensive, but this is left to your discretion. Make sure that when you do get the word out about your contests that the mechanics regarding this are simple and easily understood. There may be ordinances about raffles and promotions, so it is important to see if these are needed.

9.2 Marketing Boosts

Once you have established a marketing plan, it would be time to create the boosts that your marketing strategy needs to ensure that it reaches the maximum amount of customers in your selected area. Once you have your customers, there are several strategies that you can use to attract and keep customers coming back for more. (This should not take the place of consistently prepared and delicious food). Frequent engagement with customers through these strategies ensures that business will continue for your food truck.

- **Lighten Up, Make it Fun**

    If your food truck has a theme, such as fiestas and fair food, use this and make the atmosphere as festive as possible. Customers are more likely to visit a food truck that carries an ambience, and the theme of the food served. Not everything has to be like the restaurant business. Do whatever you can within reason to make the experience fun for your customers.

- **Customization of Orders**

    If you are accustomed to picky eaters, then this should be second nature to you. Remember that some customers may be allergic to certain ingredients. Customization of their orders may confuse the cook as well. Still, if you can accommodate these special requests, such as extra cheese, no onions, or no anchovies, then customers are more likely to patronize your business as you can provide the food that they want in the way that they like it. The main disadvantage with this, though, is that it can completely throw off your computations for your COGS and your inventory, so this strategy is highly dependent

- **Give a Behind the Scenes Look on their Favorite Foods** Some food trucks, and bustaurants (if you remember Chapter 1), have service windows on both sides of the vehicle. While this is optional, sometimes, giving the customers a peek at how their order is made can be equally fascinating and draw a crowd. This is why Sushi Bars and Benihana Restaurants are popular as customers can look at how their food is prepared. It is all about the theater of the experience. Simple gestures such as the assembling of their orders and their garnishing are enough to arouse the interests of customers. If your behind-the-scenes look is captivating enough, customers may linger and order more just to watch the show in your food truck.

- **Mobility and Location Matters**

We elaborated on the importance of location when we detailed the analysis you needed to do for your ideal location, as well as how the importance of your location can determine the profitability of your food truck. Social media would be an excellent avenue to draw customers to your location. However, knowing the right location would also help boost your visibility and other marketing strategies you employ. Popular locations to park your food truck can include sports arenas (if there is a game going on), music and art festivals, community parties, block parties, beach fronts, bars. It all depends on the locations that are available and accessible. This would also be an opportune time to ensure that you can collaborate with establishments that do not sell food so that you can feed off each other's businesses. (More on this in the next chapter)

- **Seasonality is a Good Idea to Make Them Want More**
  Seasonality makes an appearance once more, now, when it comes to food items. If you recall fast food menus, they often have limited edition items to keep customers coming back every year. While you do not have to wait that long, you can place your limited edition items on your menu as well. These can involve seasonal ingredients that make the item extra special, such as seafood, mushrooms, and fresh produce. Highlight these on your menu and social media pages to draw extra attention to them, and boost the sales of your limited edition items.
  Aside from this, you have to take into account the seasons of your area. If you happen to have a recipe for a unique ice-cold drink, break it out during the summertime to boost sales and have customers come back for more. The fall and winter months would be a great time to have a special warming food recipe as your food truck's special.

- **Linkages Promote More Business**
  In the food truck business, you will encounter competition from other food trucks and other food establishments in the area. While some may be opposed to a food truck, some would welcome the presence. Be sure to drop by these establishments and speak with their management about collaborative efforts to boost sales. An earlier example involved the pairing of a food truck and a bar that sold no food. Other examples would be a savory food truck and a dessert restaurant or café. This way, you and the restaurant can establish a mutually beneficial relationship. Business is about relationships, and cultivate these with other restaurant owners, as well as other food truck owners, who could notify you of special events in the area that they feel would be beneficial to your food truck.

10 Let Your Food Truck Be a Fixture

This chapter is the culmination of everything that the book outlined, and here, we aim to ensure that your food truck becomes a viable business for the years to come. This chapter focuses more on the need to attract customers aside from using a steady marketing plan to retain your customers and your employees.

Location Matters

In a mobile business, the location of your food truck would determine its success with the customers. Once you have done your research about a reasonable estimation of which areas in your town have the most foot traffic and have the largest population of your target demographic. However, there are a few strategies you can incorporate into your research data to ensure that your food truck maximizes all of its options.

- **Is There a Food Truck Park?**

Food truck parks are often ideal places for food truck businesses to congregate as this enables you to network with other food truck owners. More importantly, a strategic advantage with this location is that it guarantees foot traffic within the area and allows you to collaborate with other food truck owners to help enhance your business. The main disadvantage is that this is highly dependent on your location as most food truck parks are located in large cities. If you are in a more rural area, this will not work to your advantage. It is entirely possible to call and inquire about food truck parks in nearby cities and inquire about the permits needed to operate there.

- **Resourcefulness: Be Near Your Food Sources**

One of the ideal spots for a food truck would be near a market. Think about it, customers are tired from shopping, definitely hungry, and they see your food truck. It is a location that is buzzing with potential. Additionally, if you do run out of supplies, you are at a strategic advantage of having suppliers nearby for you to restock on your truck's inventory. Because you can meet your immediate suppliers, you can engage with them by featuring their product on your menu, which would get you more referrals from them. It is full of advantages. However, there may be ordinances in your area that prohibit food trucks from being parked directly next to markets and require a distance of a few meters.

- **Business Districts**

Business districts are a sure-fire way to ensure that you get foot traffic because these areas are full of people who are on their way to work. These people would surely need something to crunch on during the day. Therefore, they can purchase items from any nearby establishments. However, this has disadvantages as well, because while business districts have foot traffic, this is not constant, especially if you are in an area filled with office workers. Your sales may not be steady enough as you would have the commute rush, snack breaks, and lunch rush. After these, customers may not be interested in your food truck as they rush to go home.

- **Gas Stations**

Gas stations are great places for food trucks to park, as one, this ensures that you are near a fuel source for your generators and tanks, and two, the stream of customers would be constant since fuel is a constant need for almost everyone. This is dependent on the size of the gas stations as well as the other features they may have. Some gas stations may have their diners, and you might be construed as competition on their part, which would place you at a disadvantage. It would be best to inquire before you park.

- **Outside Watering Holes**

Watering holes and bars are more likely to not have a menu aside from bar snacks and drinks unless they happen to be a gastropub. It is always a good idea to call these bars and ask them if it is possible to park outside their establishment, especially if they serve no food. This way, you both collaborate, with you supplying the food and them supplying the drinks. As mentioned in the previous chapter, this is an exercise in collaboration. Gourmet food trucks would enjoy these areas, as customers would want to look for a food truck that offers rich street food options. This, however, limits your sale time from late afternoon to early morning.

- **Gravitate towards Large Events**

Large events such as festivals and shows are a great draw for crowds, and there are two possibilities here for your food truck. You can park nearby and ensure a steady stream of food for all the attendees of the event, or you can negotiate with the event organizers for exclusivity rights to sell food for the event. You will need to have your permits for the latter option. You can also cater for the event if you can get advanced notice, so you do not become short on ingredients. Keep your ear out on the latest events in your area as well as nearby areas.

- **Colleges: Never a Bad Idea**

Parking a food truck near college campuses is an easy way to cater to the needs of the students. However, because most of them are on a budget, your meals would have to be delicious, filling, and inexpensive to make your food truck worth the student's while. This makes up for it, though, by the sheer volume of customers, especially if you are in a college town.

10.1 Think Long-Term

At this point, the food truck is well into its first month or so in operations, and you need to envision long-term plans that will keep your food truck a successful and viable business for years to come.

- **Be Flexible, Be Adaptive to the Needs and Demands of the Customers**

  Listen to what your customers want, and accommodate them within reason if possible. This goes beyond the customization of orders, as mentioned in the previous chapter. This refers to keeping your pulse on what your customers need, whether it is a warm meal or a more inexpensive meal due to the economic downturn experienced in this pandemic. This aside, when you listen to your customers, you can identify areas for improvement. This can include the need to streamline prep time if customers are unable to wait for their food, as an example. This indicates to the customer that not only do you listen, but you are changing to accommodate their needs. They will appreciate your food truck more.

- **Reserve Funds for the Rainy Days**
Somedays might look dull, and you need to understand that every day won't be a rainy day. So, learn to prepare your mindset for unforeseen circumstances. To avoid any unforeseen financial constraints and unexpected emergencies in the business, you must be able to save the profits from the business for times when your food truck needs it the most (repairs, emergency maintenance, etc.). To ensure that this does not cut into your profits and make you shell out personal funds to answer for these emergencies.

- **Be Unique, Stand Out and Make a Trend**
This mostly refers to the branding and visibility of the food truck, and in the long run, you will want to think of newer ways to stand out from other food trucks now that the initial buzz has been accomplished. Engage with the community, think of unique marketing styles that could generate more hype about your business to ensure a continuous flow of customers.

- **Provide Great Service**
When you create a food truck business, you can provide great service in every aspect, from taking down orders to food preparation. Earlier in this book, we discussed menu plans and consistencies, and by this point, your employees know how to make the standard dishes that your food truck sells. Great service implies consistency in preparing and selling your products which should always be of the same quality from the minute the food truck first opened its windows to sell. Customers will keep on coming back for more if your food trucks provide the same quality of food sold with the same quality of service they had received when they began visiting your food truck.

- **Frequent Communication**

Simply put, this means you need to establish a more open line of communication between yourself and your employees and yourself and your suppliers. Frequent communication helps iron out any potential concerns that may arise as the food truck operates. Similarly, frequently communicate with your customers to update them on the latest news from your business.

- **Keep an Eye on Costs**

  The profitability of your food truck hinges upon the costs needed for the food, labor, and maintenance of the truck and its kitchen. Throughout the book, various formulae were given to help you identify if your truck is turning out a profit and identifying weak sellers in your menu that you can cut out and replace with dishes that can generate better sales. With the fluctuation of priceS, you must keep a close eye on your COGS and other expenses that your food truck can incur.

Grow Your Business

Progress is a sign that your business is flourishing, and with this, you can think about growing your business. In Chapter 2, we discussed the financial options available for your food truck should you wish to expand the number of food trucks you operate in your area. While the same rules apply to the establishment of your food truck, you can recoup the costs with the number of sales that you can make in a single day. If you experience a high demand for the products that your food truck sells, then adding another truck to your business would be a viable option. However, this is dependent on the demand for your product and your financials.

- There are potential advantages here, especially when you purchase supplies for your food trucks if you choose to expand. If you purchase more supplies in bulk, you can obtain bigger discounts which could lower your overall COGS, and cause you to lower your prices or obtain more profits from every order made. Compute for your overall food costs to determine which course of action you should take.

- Because another truck has been added, you may find an increase in the amount of fuel you will need, as well as insurance costs and maintenance costs for your food truck.

Your food truck can venture into other businesses, which includes the catering of small events. Food truck owners need to remember that they need to negotiate with their clients and have it in writing. You can always say no if you feel that you are unable to meet the customer's requirements; this protects you from negative reviews.

As with a food truck, you may choose to begin a new brick-and-mortar business if you'd like. The only reason you haven't started a food truck is because you want to avoid dealing with the challenges that come with it.

Think of the Customers

At the heart of it all, your customers, or by this time, your patrons are at the heart of your business, and while they are not directly involved in the operations of the food truck, they are what help keep your business afloat. Strategies to retain them are always a good idea to improve your relationship with them.

- **Loyalty Programs for Best Customers**
  You have probably seen systems that reward customers for their patronage, and there is no reason why the same concept cannot be applied to your food truck. It is bad business practice to constantly give freebies to your customers as this will lead them to want more and more, which can cut into your costs to offset the amount spent on the freebies. You can start with the simplest idea, which involves using a card where if a customer purchases a specific order, they get a sticker on the card, and if they collect enough, they get a reward. This is similar to what Starbucks employs for their yearly planners.

- **Draft a Tier System**
  Tiered Reward Systems are ideal for customers who do not frequent your food truck as much as you would like to. In exchange for their repeat business, your food truck can offer items of greater value according to how often they visit. Simple items like a free drink if they visit at least thrice a year; up to a

free meal if customers visit more than ten times. Similarly, you can use a points system, where every purchase the customer makes accumulates a certain number of points. The more points a customer accumulates, the higher the rewards they can get. For this approach, you would need a system that can keep a tally of the number of points each customer has.

10.2 Exiting the Food Truck Business

There comes a time when you feel that you would not be able to continue the food truck business, and at some point, you may want to exit the business altogether. There are various reasons for this which can include:

- You feel that the food truck business is no longer fun as you thought it would be. This is a perfectly acceptable reason in the same way burnout is a reason to quit a career.
- You feel that the food truck takes a lot of investment, and you do not want to initiate the steps needed to expand your food truck.
- You feel overwhelmed with the tasks needed to keep the food truck operational, and you cannot keep up.

These are some reasons why food truck owners quit the business, but before you decide to close up shop for good, there are a few steps.

- Ensure that all your documentation is in order; these include your profit and loss statements for the past three years, balance sheets and tax returns from the past three years, a list of equipment and their estimated value with accommodations for depreciation, and your list of inventories. These ensure that you come up with a reasonable price to sell your business to other interested parties.
- Business brokers may ease the negotiations between you and prospective buyers. Consult with your attorney and accountant to see if they have anyone they can recommend to broker a reasonable deal between you and your buyer.

11 Conclusion

Throughout the ten chapters of this book, you have learned about the intricacies of what the food truck business is actually like from the perspective of a food truck owner. This is vastly different from seeing the food truck through the eyes of the customer. Behind every success story of a food truck owner lies the culmination of several years' worth of planning, financing, research, and groundwork for a food truck owner to run the food truck. Even the creation of a food truck has its own steps, as you would have to know what you want to establish in the business and what you need to be able to achieve it. In this book as well, you learned about the necessary miscellaneous requirements for you to hire your employees and how to look for the best professionals. They can help you run your business, the suppliers you will need, and the steps you can take to protect your business. Lastly, while the food truck operates, this book discussed how you could make your food truck grow through the use of marketing strategies and rewards for your customers, as well as generating the hype your business needs. Conversely, it also focuses on how you can let it go should the time come for you to sell your truck. Thank you for reading this book, and we hope this helps you on your journey to be a successful food truck owner.

Contact and Thanks

In this book, I have included all the knowledge, strategies and solutions I have learned in my food truck business career. I hope you have enjoyed this publication which took me months of work and sacrifices. Thank you for reading this book, I admit it was not easy to make this publication. I hope it will be useful to you and I would be happy to receive your opinion with an unbiased and honest review, it would mean a lot to me and help me to improve in future publications.

Reference

- Feedback on food truck app! : foodtrucks. www.reddit.com/r/foodtrucks/comments/jbzxcz/feedback_on_food_truck_app/
- www.smamarketing.net/blog/direct-sales-business-using-inbound-marketing
- 7 Challenges Food Truck Owners Must Overcome | Complete www.completecontroller.com/7-challenges-food-truck-owners-must-overcome/
- Leaving a will of legacy | Business Observer | Business .... www.businessobserverfl.com/article/leaving-will-legacy
- Solved: "There Is No Such Thing As A Fixed Cost. All Costs. www.chegg.com/homework-help/questions-and-answers/thing-fixed-cost-costs-unfixed-given-sufficient-time-agree-implication-answer-cvp-analysis-q59584514
- Guide to Opening Your First Restaurant. www.tabakinsurance.com/info/guide-to-opening-your-first-restaurant/
- Aspects you should consider to start a restaurant. www.eastroomchicago.com/aspects-you-should-consider-to-start-a-restaurant/

- Get every Type of Food Truck Business Plan from Us. www.studybay.com/food-truck-business-plan/
- Online Lead Generation Blog | marketing planning. www.collaborativegrowthnetwork.com/blog/topic/marketing-planning
- Online Lead Generation Blog | marketing planning. www.collaborativegrowthnetwork.com/blog/topic/marketing-planning
- Online Lead Generation Blog | marketing planning. www.collaborativegrowthnetwork.com/blog/topic/marketing-planning
- Does a Single Member LLC Need an EIN? | Nolo. www.nolo.com/legal-encyclopedia/does-single-member-llc-need-ein.html
- 1993 Inst W-2 - IRS. www.irs.gov/pub/irs-prior/iw2--1993.pdf
- How to File a Tax Return When You Have 1099 Income From www.businessinsider.com/personal-finance/tax-return-help-1099-income-freelance-2019-2
- Documents Needed for Mortgage Application | Guaranteed Rate. www.rate.com/resources/documents-you-will-need-to-apply-for-a-home-mortgage
- Bickel, Amy. "Host of Issues Clogging Aqueduct Idea." The Hutchinson News, Hutchinson News, 19 Mar. 2015, p. n/a.
- Bickel, Amy. "Host of Issues Clogging Aqueduct Idea." The Hutchinson News, Hutchinson News, 19 Mar. 2015, p. n/a.
- How to develop a recruitment plan | Workable. www.resources.workable.com/tutorial/develop-recruitment-plan
- Create a Culture of Responsibility | Inc.com. www.inc.com/peter-economy/create-culture-of-responsibility.html
- Create a Culture of Responsibility | Inc.com. www.inc.com/peter-economy/create-culture-of-responsibility.html
- Customer power: How to deal with online complaints - Teal www.tbccpa.com/resources/articles/customer-power-how-to-deal-with-online-complaints/
- Keep Food Safe from Store to Storage: Shopping Food Safety www.ag.ndsu.edu/publications/food-nutrition/keep-food-safe-from-store-to-storage-shopping-food-safety-facts
- Sodium Nitrate Vs. Sodium Nitrite | Healthy Eating | SF Gate. www.healthyeating.sfgate.com/sodium-nitrate-vs-sodium-nitrite-9064.html

- Hepatitis C is emerging health crisis related to opioid ....
  www.hepatitiscmsg.org/blog/hepatitis-c-is-emerging-health-crisis-related-to-opioid-addiction
- How to Keep Hamburgers Warm After Cooking Them ....
  www.livestrong.com/article/544982-how-to-keep-hamburgers-warm-after-cooking-them/
- Four food safety guests to invite to your party - MSU ....
  www.canr.msu.edu/news/four_food_safety_guests_to_invite_to_your_party
- HFS 3757 Medicare Savings for Qualified Beneficiaries.
  www.illinois.gov/hfs/info/Brochures%20and%20Forms/Brochures/Pages/HFS3757.aspx
- www.wikihow.com/Start-a-Website-Business
- www.our.utah.edu/wp-content/uploads/sites/19/2019/05/jabini.pdf
- www.coursehero.com/file/96635022/Individual-Reportediteddocx/
- Online Marketing Tutorial: How To Set Up Your Online ....
  www.wealthmagnate.com/online-marketing-tutorial/
- www.pos.toasttab.com/blog/on-the-line/how-to-calculate-food-cost-percentage
- www.web.archive.org/web/20180712180000/http://www.co.sibley.mn.us:80/GuideToSTARTINGABUSINESSINMINNESOTA2015.pdf
- www.businessnewsdaily.com/9237-how-to-start-food-truck-business.html
- www.fitsmallbusiness.com/how-to-start-a-food-truck/
- www.webstaurantstore.com/article/54/how-write-food-truck-business-plan.html
- www.irs.com/articles/information-for-irs-tax-form-w-2
- www.cyrusmehta.com/blog/2019/07/01/immigration-update-july-1-2019/
- www.web.archive.org/web/20080723163136/http://www.btikansas.com/sbdc/busplan.html
- www.igi-global.com/gateway/chapter/276193
- www.iclg.com/practice-areas/employment-and-labour-laws-and-regulations/india
- www.kobra.uni-kassel.de/bitstream/handle/123456789/12167/kup_9783737608930.pdf?isAllowed=y&sequence=6
- www.inc.com/peter-economy/create-culture-of-responsibility.html

141

- www.openmyfloridabusiness.gov/wp-content/uploads/2020/01/OMFB-eGuide.pdf
- www.smartasset.com/mortgage/what-is-a-business-mortgage
- www.onlinelibrary.wiley.com/doi/book/10.1002/9781119510369
- www.healthyeating.sfgate.com/sodium-nitrate-vs-sodium-nitrite-9064.html
- www.mobile-cuisine.com/business-plan/food-truck-financial-expenses-business-plan/
- www.rmagazine.com/articles/understanding-food-cost-and-how-to-budget.html
- www.urgentbusinessforms.com/wp-content/uploads/2017/09/Employee-Handbook-Sample.pdf
- www.ag.ndsu.edu/publications/food-nutrition/keep-food-safe-from-store-to-storage-shopping-food-safety-facts
- www.insureon.com/food-business-insurance/food-trucks/cost
- www.eu.thedailyjournal.com/story/opinion/columnists/2017/12/11/hepatitis-c-health-crisis-opioid-tennessee/907512001/
- www.profitableventure.com/vegan-food-truck-business-plan/
- Shaima Azam (2020), Nanu Bari: F Anu Bari: For People Who Love Desi F e Desi Food – and Their ood – and Their Grandma: A Food Truck Business Plan, www.digitalcommons.salemstate.edu/cgi/viewcontent.cgi?article=1271&context=honors_theses
- Angelo A. Camillo. "Managerial Accounting for Non-Accountants in Restaurant Operations." Strategic International Restaurant Development: From Concept to Production, IGI Global, 2021, pp.206-304. http://doi:10.4018/978-1-7998-4342-9.ch008
- Russell Fox (2013), Tax Strategies for the Small Business Owner, Springer.

CPSIA information can be obtained
at www.ICGtesting.com
Printed in the USA
BVHW050544140223
658474BV00023B/359